GEORGE CLOONEY

THIS IS A CARLTON BOOK

Published in 2008 by Carlton Books Limited
20 Mortimer Street
London W1T 3JW

10 9 8 7 6 5 4 3 2 1

Text and design copyright © Carlton Books Limited 2008

The right of Shana Cushman to be identified as the author of
this work has been asserted by her in accordance with the
Copyright, Designs and Patents Act 1988.

A CIP catalogue record for this book is available from the
British Library.

ISBN 978-1-84732-145-9

Editorial Manager: Rod Green
Cover Designer: Katie Baxendale
Designer: Gülen Shevki-Taylor
Picture Research: Paul Langan
Production: Claire Hayward

Printed in Dubai

GEORGE CLOONEY

AN ILLUSTRATED BIOGRAPHY SHANA CUSHMAN

CARLTON
BOOKS

CONTENTS

SaveDarfur.org

INTRODUCTION

Great actor. Great director. Acclaimed writer, producer. Maverick talent.
Charmer. Idealist. Rebel. Ladies man. Man's man. Baseball and basketball
enthusiast. Social and political activist. Master of the self-deprecatory
quip. Approachable. Old fashioned. Fiercely private. The new Cary Grant.
"Sexiest Man Alive". Reluctant pin-up. Hollywood all-rounder. These are
some of the things that come to mind when you consider the life and
career of George Clooney. Oh, and, of course, the infamous mischievous
grin that has had women from one end of the world to the other going
weak at the knees for years.

A cross more than two decades, he has slowly climbed the ladder of success, rung by rung, with boundless energy, patience and commitment. His story is not one of overnight success. He started out in TV, scraping a living, taking any part that came his way. He first found success playing "George Burnett" in American TV show, *The Facts Of Life*, between 1985-87. He was in his mid twenties by then. Other bit parts circled the stability of being a regular on a TV show.

Then, in 1988, he landed the role of "Booker Brooks" on *Roseanne*. For the next three years, his good looks, weary-wise demeanour, trademark sultry-paternal deep voice and macho-vulnerable emotional make-up would win the hearts of millions of viewers.

During that time, his reputation in bloom, he set his sights on bucking a long-standing Hollywood rule of thumb, which says TV stars tend not to be able to cross over to Hollywood and strike it equally big as movie stars. The regularity of a series brands the actor or actress with the character they play. Audiences who love those characters, tend to become possessive and dislike seeing the actors and actresses behind those characters, playing new roles in other TV shows or feature films.

Beyond that, whenever George read for parts in feature films, he tended to find himself tagged as being too much of a TV actor. Most famously he was turned down for the part of "J.D." in Ridley Scott's 1991 film, *Thelma and*

Louise, in favour of Brad Pitt.

When his involvement with *Roseanne* came to an end, he moved on to two further successful roles, in the TV shows, *Bodies of Evidence* (1992-93) and *Sisters* (1993-94). All the while, he kept auditioning for feature films but never won any parts. And then, in a stroke of good luck, he landed the role that would catapult him to international fame as a TV star.

The show was medical drama, *E.R.* and George was to play "Dr Doug Ross", that suave yet flawed, passionate yet chaotic hero of a doctor. Between 1994 and 1999, he would mesmerise TV audiences through 108 luminous episodes. His departure, arguably, marked the zenith of the show's potency.

Upon finding fame as Dr Ross, he focussed his sights ever more on breaking into Hollywood. The much-prayed-for break came when George landed the part of "Seth Gecko" in Roberto Rodriguez' 1996 film, *From Dusk Till Dawn*. The screenplay was written by then golden boy Quentin Tarantino, who also acted in the film, alongside George, Harvey Keitel, Salma Hayek and Juliette Lewis. The company of method actor heavyweight Keitel and hip director Tarantino lent George industry kudos and heralded a new era in which his public reputation as Dr Ross/a TV star, was slowly tweaked until he was recast in the public consciousness as an actor, director, writer and producer – a Hollywood all-rounder – of tremendous integrity.

Having safely crossed over to Hollywood and built a reputation as a movie star via roles in films such as *One Fine Day, The Peacemaker, Batman and Robin, Out Of Sight, The Thin Red Line* and *Three Kings*, George felt confident enough to leave *E.R.* in 1999, waving goodbye to his career as a TV actor for good.

Set free from the little screen, George kept up a furious work pace, delivering acclaimed performances in *O Brother Where Art Thou?, Solaris, Ocean's Eleven* and *Syriana*.

In tandem, having already started working as a producer, George, ever ambitious, set his sights on a new goal: directing a feature film. He realised this ambition in 2002, with *Confessions Of A Dangerous Mind*. Since then, he has directed two further features - *Good Night And Good Luck* and *Leatherheads* - and acted in further acclaimed films such as *The Good German*, *Ocean's Twelve*, *Ocean's Thirteen*, *Michael Clayton* and *Burn After Reading*.

He continues to maintain a prolific output, a man with many fingers in many different pies. Parallel to the professional accomplishments and acclaim, his private life, much to his distaste, continues to fascinate the media, which pays particular and persistent attention to his romantic life. A man's man linked with many women since coming to fame with *E.R.*, George has kept the media guessing by maintaining a reputation as Hollywood's most eligible bachelor.

He was once married to actress Talia Balsam, but the couple underwent a painful divorce in 1992. Since then, George has stated over and over that he will never marry again or have children. It has become part of his persona – so much so that actresses Michelle Pfeiffer and Nicole Kidman each bet him $10,000 that he would settle down by the age of forty. When that milestone came around in 2001, they had to send their cheques to George. With characteristic humour, he returned both cheques, with a note to each actress changing the stakes to double or nothing if he still hadn't settled down by fifty.

Today, George Clooney is still Hollywood's most eligible bachelor and one of Tinseltown's most powerful figures. Holding steady at the top of his game, he remains that rare thing – a TV star turned movie star. And yet rarer still – a TV star turned movie star, turned savvy producer, turned acclaimed director and writer. Add to that, in recent years, the fact that George has used his power and influence to champion social and political causes about which he feels strongly. Despite all of these accomplishments, George remains astonishingly prolific and driven and it seems unlikely that his white-hot status in Hollywood will cool any time soon.

Above: George and Brad Pitt looking cool in the sunshine on the set of *Ocean's Eleven*.

Below: George sported a "Clarke Gable" moustache in *O Brother Where Art Thou?*

1

THE EARLY YEARS

George Timothy Clooney was born on 6 May 1961 in Lexington, Kentucky.
He was the second child born to Nick and Nina Clooney. A year earlier,
Nina had given birth to a daughter, Ada Clooney, on 2 May. Nick Clooney
met Nina Warren when he was emcee at a local Miss Lexington beauty
pageant. Later that day, he asked Nina out on a date. Hitting it off, the
couple started dating and soon after Nick asked Nina to marry him.

"YOU'RE A
MEMBER OF
THE WORLD
COMMUNITY.
NEVER
FORGET
WHERE YOU
PUT YOUR
HANDS IN
THE WATER."

Nina Bruce Warren was born in Boyle County, Kentucky, on 24 August 1939, to Marvin Jackson Warren and Dica Mae Edwards. Nick Clooney was born Nicholas Joseph Clooney on 13 January 1934 in Maysville, Kentucky, to Andrew Joseph Clooney and Frances Guilfoyle Clooney. The roots of both families harked back to Ireland. Emigration to the United States is believed to have happened in either the 1860s or 1870s.

Nick's sisters, Rosemary and Betty Clooney, were both singers. Their hard-drinking father painted houses for a living. Their paternal grandfather, Andrew J. Clooney was a jeweller and at one time the Mayor of Maysville, on the Democrat ticket. When Nick was four, his parents separated. His father relocated to Washington D.C. and his mother found work in a dress shop in Lexington, the children spending much of their time with their grandparents.

As a child, Nick was fascinated by reporters on the radio, breaking news about the Second World War. He particularly liked Edward R. Murrow, Elmer Davis and William Shirer.

One day, his grandfather took him and his sisters down to the banks of the Ohio River and instructed them to kneel down and put their hands in the water. He explained to them the journey of that river, how eventually it reached the Atlantic. The young Nick listened as his grandfather told them, "You're a member of the world community. Never forget where you put your hands in the water."

Such touching sentiments have stayed with Nick his whole life. He went into broadcast journalism in 1951, following in the footsteps of his hero, Edward R. Murrow. He got a job working for the Maysville radio station, WFTM, before he went into the army, climbing to the rank of Corporal.

When he got out of the army, he moved to California, thinking he might become an actor. His sister, Rosemary Clooney, was a famous singer by then and married to the actor and director, Jose Ferrer. She also added acting to her accomplishments, starting with a 1951 appearance on *The Bob Hope Show*. In 1953, she had made her feature film debut in *The Stars Are Shining* and in 1956, began hosting her own TV show, *The Rosemary Clooney Show*.

Nick, by comparison, was struggling. He made a fleeting appearance in Ferrer's 1958 comedy, *The High Cost of Living*, playing 'man in parking lot' and acted in small theatre productions, even appearing in a dog food commercial. Eventually, money became tight and, sensing his acting career wasn't going the way he hoped, he packed his bags to return to Kentucky.

Nick settled in Lexington, a small city, whose population today is estimated at around 270,000. First settled in 1775, Lexington sits 45 miles (72 km) from Louisville and 47 miles (76 km) from Cincinnati. Famous for horse racing and tobacco, the city underwent an economic boom in the 1950s when corporations such as IBM opened major offices and manufacturing plants there.

Soon after arriving back, Nick met Nina Warren at that beauty pageant. They were married on 13 August 1959, days shy of her twentieth birthday. When their second child was born in 1961, they named him George after his great uncle George Guilfoyle, who flew numerous missions with the U.S. Air Force against the Nazis during the Second World War.

Previous spread:
George's father, Nick Clooney, spinning discs for the U.S. Army's Armed Forces Network in Frankfurt, Germany, while in the Army in 1956.
Right: George with his mother, Nina, at the *Ocean's Thirteen* premiere in Los Angeles in 2007.
Far right: George's Aunt, Rosemary Clooney, had a glittering career as a singing star a full decade before George was born in 1961.

George was born into a talented and ambitious, liberal family. His father was now working as a news anchor for WKYT. His Aunt Rosemary was a singing star, as well as a TV presenter and actress. His other Aunt, Betty, was also known as a singer. And then, there was Rosemary's husband, Jose Ferrer, an actor and director. He grew up surrounded by talent inseparable from a public life. This couldn't fail to influence George, as he later told *The New York Times*: "In that world, I was famous from the time I was born."

The family had strict values. "I had a very strict family," George later told *Parade*. "My father's a big liberal Democrat, but that doesn't mean he was liberal in any way with his kids. My mother was easier than my father, but both were tough disciplinarians. My parents had immense confidence in their own and their kids' abilities. You always felt you'd succeed if you did things for the right reasons."

George started school at the Blessed Sacrament Elementary School in Fort Mitchell, Kentucky, a co-ed Roman Catholic school. When he was five, the family left Lexington and moved to Cincinnati, Ohio, where his father, following in his sister Rosemary's footsteps, launched *The Nick Clooney Show* for WLWC. George was then enrolled at St Michael's school in Columbus, Ohio and then at Western Row Elementary school in Mason, Ohio.

Then Nick's show moved to WKRC and George was transferred to St Susanna Elementary School, in Mason, Ohio. He would study there for five years, all the way to high school. An extension of the local parish church, the school has a strong Catholic identity.

It was quite common for Nick to take his family to work. The whole family tended to muck in, one for all and all for one. "By the time I was five," George later told *Parade*. "I was always on my dad's variety show. My mom did audience bits. I worked the cue cards, did skits and commercials. My sister worked, too. It was like Andy Hardy: My family put on a show."

His father was constantly juggling engagements. George has said that his father typically made around 200 personal appearances at public functions per year and that the entire Clooney clan tended to feature in the act. "We'd be fighting in the car on the way over, but when we'd get out of the car and people would shout, 'Nick!' and ask for autographs, we'd have our arms around each other, smiling. After the show, we'd get back in the car and sulk all the way home. I understood there is the real you and the public persona. Two different people."

When Nina was working, George and Ada would go into work with their father. "Often," George later said, "the newsroom would be our babysitter. My sister and I would hang out with my dad and all these smart journalists. I remember watching them in discussion. They were so inspiring that I never forgot it."

The Clooneys lived an Irish-American Catholic life and attended church. George has described them as "Catholic, big time, whole family." He even served as an altar boy, which involved extensive participation in the ceremonial aspects of Mass.

George was, by all accounts, a good-natured child, known for his sense of humour. His mother later told *The Cincinnati Enquirer* that she and Nick thought he might end up being a stand-up comedian.

Above: Nick Clooney hosting *The Money Maze* TV game show in 1975.
Left: Rosemary Clooney with her husband, actor and director Jose Ferrer.

In 1969, aged eight, according to his mother, George was diagnosed with dyslexia. Nina had suffered from it as a child, too, before growing out of it. History repeated itself and George was also to shake off the condition as he grew older.

When he was ten, he made his TV debut, in costume. "My father had a variety show on a local television station during the last years of live TV," George later told *Playboy*. "So, for us, I remember this room that had all these character costumes in it. We were like a Vaudeville family. I was ten years old and it would be St. Patrick's Day, and my dad would interview me. I'd dress up like a leprechaun and I'd have a cigar and he'd say, 'What's it like being a leprechaun?'"

In December 1974, the family moved to Augusta, Kentucky and George was enrolled at Augusta High School. In his first year at that high school, he started exhibiting symptoms of what was quickly diagnosed as Bell's Palsy.

The illness, which causes facial muscles to weaken or become temporarily paralysed, is believed to affect approximately 0.02 per cent of the American population. According to the National Institute of Neurological Disorders and Stroke (NINDS), typical symptoms include, "twitching, weakness, or paralysis on one or both sides of the face, drooping of the eyelid and corner of the mouth, drooling, dryness of the eye or mouth, impairment of taste, and excessive tearing in one eye."

There are no concrete theories as to what brings on a case of Bell's Palsy and in most cases, after the initial onset, symptoms calm down within a fortnight and tend to disappear altogether within nine months.

The first symptoms took hold in a peculiar chain of events. One day, George watched the 1942 film *The Pride Of The Yankees* on TV. In the film, Gary Cooper's character falls sick with Lou Gehrig's disease. In one particular scene, which made an impression on George, he picks up a bat but as he does so, he loses his grip and it falls from his hand.

The next day, the Clooneys were attending mass in church, sitting in the pews, when George's tongue went completely numb. After Church, as per family routine, they went for dinner at a restaurant called Frisch's Big Boy.

There, while drinking a glass of milk, George was unable to keep control over the way he drank and milk came gushing from his mouth. Alarmed, he immediately thought of Gary Cooper in the film he'd seen the day before and panicked that he was succumbing to Lou Gehrig's disease.

In 1974, when George was thirteen, Nick became a familiar face to millions of Americans when he hosted the ABC game show, *The Money Maze*. Overnight, George developed a certain celebrity at school, his father's fame now adding to that of his hugely successful Aunt Rosemary.

Whether his father was on TV and radio or not, he never stopped working excessively hard, going from job to job, project to project. George would inherit this work ethic, this intense fear of work drying up. He told *The Los Angeles Times* in 1997 what it was like growing up in house with a father who went from one contract to the next, the future ever uncertain: "We didn't grow up in trailers, although we did

that we would hear from and we'd go out and buy presents for them. We involved our kids in what we were doing, although some of it may have been not having a babysitter to leave them with. Until they were 15 or 16 years old, they went with us almost everywhere."

That changed in 1977, when George passed his driving test and was able to hit the road in a car independently.

In his early teens, he showed promise at both basketball and baseball – two games he loved. In 1977, George managed to try out for the Cincinnati Reds baseball team. At the time, the team's star players included Pete Rose, whom George has namechecked in interviews. Despite massive enthusiasm for the game and a passable talent, he never made it past that first try-out. Surrounded by the game's best players, George realized he wasn't outstanding. "When I realized I was never going to be those guys," he said later, "I could walk away because I'd at least given it a run. My greatest skill is probably understanding my own limitations."

In 1979, George graduated from Augusta High School. He had not been a particularly spectacular student in academic terms, but had always ranked high in any activity relating to sports. "We didn't have a football team at Augusta High," he later said. "Too small a school. So I played varsity baseball and basketball. Those were my sports. Actually, we only had two sports. I think we had a track team one year, but that was it. No tennis team, no nothing."

When it came to American football, George supported the Cincinnati Bengals. But a passion for the Bengals and the Reds didn't amount to a career now that he had graduated from high school. Nor did watching Spencer Tracy movies on TV. He considered various possibilities before deciding to follow in his father's footsteps and applying for a place studying Broadcast Journalism at Northern Kentucky University. He was accepted to the university, which was founded in 1968. It seemed like a first step. All he knew was that he didn't want to go into adulthood

Above: In 1977, George's talent for baseball led to trials with the Cincinnati Reds.

move around when the rent was due. We'd vacillate from my dad having a very good job to being unemployed."

Around the same time, George agreed to dress up in an Easter Bunny costume for his father's TV show. But then, once he was dressed, at home, ready to do it, nature intervened. As George told *The Los Angeles Times* in 1997, "I think I was 13 and I was at home trying on the costume in Kentucky where I lived and the ground started shaking. It was the first earthquake Augusta had had in 150 years. Things were flying and I was running out in these giant feet and full bunny outfit on a Sunday afternoon yelling, 'What the hell's going on?!'"

All the while, the Clooneys raised Ada and George to share the same experiences, as Nina Warren Clooney told *Cincinnati Parent* in 2007: "We were always doing events for charities and certainly at Christmas time, there were several families

known only for being a relative of Nick and Rosemary Clooney.

George didn't take well to student life and, far from thriving in the academic arena, he has said that he was instead "really good at drinking." Unsurprisingly, he didn't stay the course and dropped out. With no idea about what he was going to with his life, his immediate headache was money. He took a part-time job working at a menswear store called Nadler's Mens Clothing in Kenwood Mall.

His manager was called James E. Marshall Jr. and his wife, Pat Marshall, told Cincinnati.com in 2006, that her husband used to lay on a festive buffet in the store's back office every Christmas. The Christmas George worked there, she went to the party and met George's mother, Nina. Everyone who worked at the store knew George as Nick Clooney's son, the very thing that George would rather have avoided.

Before long, George left Nadler's Mens Clothing and started a new job. A large department store, McAlpin's, had opened on 29 July 1979, in Crestview Hills Mall. George landed a position working in the shoe department. He was hired by the then Human Resources Director, Sally Gravett. In a feature on Cincinnati.com in 2006, she elaborated, explaining that George was a model, good humoured employee, whose primary work involved selling shoes, unpacking new deliveries of shoes and putting them out on display.

Other former colleagues also spoke highly of George in the feature. According to Virginia Schwartz, George was "a cut-up and prankster" but "very nice to the older ladies that came in to buy shoes." Lisa Henderson recalls that George was "always smiling, joking and snoozing on the job" and that once, he was "found napping in the dressing room during work hours." Nancy

Above: George studied Broadcast Journalism at Northern Kentucky University.

Above: George with
his cousin Miguel
Ferrer, the man who
first suggested that
George take up a
career in acting.
Right: Rosemary
Clooney and Jose
Ferrer with their
children, Monsita,
Rafael, Miguel, Maria
and Gabriel.

Selby offered a more sociable portrait, "We were young and would hang out at the bars together." George, it seems, was charming and well-liked by his colleagues and customers, but hardly committed to a career in shoe retailing.

In spring 1981, Rosemary Clooney's ex-husband, Jose Ferrer and two of their sons, Miguel and Rafi, with whom George had grown up, arrived in Kentucky to shoot a horse racing film in Lexington. George told *Esquire* in 2008 that he loaned his car, a Monte Carlo, to the Ferrers and received $50 a day as a rental tab. They also invited him to appear in the film, whose working title was *And They're Off*, as an extra. He tagged along, appeared as an extra and fell head over heels in love with the profession of acting.

This meant he would once more drop out of university. George had decided to give the academic realm another shot and was enrolled at the University of Cincinnati. His father told him that dropping out was a bad idea, that he needed to complete his studies so that he'd have something to fall back on if the acting didn't work out. George told his father that if he had something to fall back on, then he'd simply fall back. He did not want the comfort of a "safety net". And that was that, George dropped out of the

University of Cincinnati, having lasted what his mother later described "maybe two minutes."

During the *And They're Off* shoot, George spent three months sleeping on and off on the sofa in Miguel's hotel room. It had been Miguel who suggested that George move to Los Angeles and devote his life to making it as an actor. George, of course, had needed little encouragement and to begin planning his move. Little did he know that the impressions of the acting life he had culled from working on *And They're Off*, were shaky, to say the very least. The film would never be released.

In summer 1981, George, his sights firmly set on an acting career, took any work he could find in a bid to roll up enough cash to make the trip to California. Taking advantage of growing up in one of the largest tobacco-producing regions in the world, he got a job cutting tobacco. The work was hard, the labour made all the heavier by the Clooney family's unfortunate relationship with tobacco products – George has said that eight of his uncles and aunts died between the ages of sixty and seventy from complications arising from smoking.

More healthily, he sold lemonade in Augusta when the annual Labor Day festival came around. And he carried on working at McAlpin's. Once he had saved up, George told Sally Gravett that he would be leaving McAlpin's for good. Everybody he had worked with, including Gravett, was sad to see him go. At home, he packed his belongings. He had saved up $450 from his assorted jobs – enough to make a go of his dream.

With those savings in his pocket, in Autumn 1981, he climbed into his clapped out 1976 model Monte Carlo and hit the highway. The destination was Los Angeles, where he would be staying with his Aunt Rosemary until he could get a foot in the door of the acting world. Three days later, he pulled into the driveway of her Beverly Hills home and began his new life.

2

THE FACTS OF LIFE

The first thing that had to go was the car. His Aunt Rosemary would simply not tolerate George's rusty banger sitting on the driveway of her Beverly Hills home. That non-negotiable hiccup out the way, George set about helping his Aunt, in return for a bed and roof over his head, until he could find work as an actor. "Helping" entailed doing handyman jobs around the house but mostly working as chauffeur to Rosemary and her friends and colleagues. George took the driver's seat when Rosemary, Kaye Ballard, Martha Raye and Helen O'Connell, struck out on their 4 Girls 4 tour.

He later reminisced fondly about the tour in an interview with ukhollywood.com, "I was twenty and it was a lot of fun. They were always drinking, laughing, smoking and trashing everyone they knew. They were tough old broads and I loved them."

Once he found his feet, he packed his bags and moved into a small apartment occupied by fellow aspiring actor and friend, Thom Matthews. George, strapped for cash, famously set up camp in Matthews' walk-in closet, literally occupying no more than that tiny, confined space. His bed was a bunk-bed mattress, laid inside the floor of the walk-in closet. This severely compromised living situation displayed George's utmost determination to make it as an actor, regardless of whatever hardships that might come with such an ambitious pursuit of such an elusive line of work.

This cramped living arrangement would last for eight months. George has referred to that era since as the "greatest time of my life", indicating that it wasn't all toil, living hand to mouth and compromise.

Matthews, born in November 1958, was 23 at the time. He had decided to pursue acting after a girlfriend suggested it. Today, Matthews co-owns the construction firm, Hammer and Trowel Construction and continues to act. He and George have remained friends and Matthews is a key figure in George's infamously tight circle of male friends – known as 'the Boys'.

Matthews got his first break as an actor when he landed a part playing a paramedic in an episode of hit US TV show, *Falconcrest*, in 1982. A year later, he appeared in two episodes of the equally popular US TV show, *Dynasty*, credited as "male secretary". It is possible that Matthews led George to TV. Years later, in 1995, when George had become a household name in *E.R.*, Matthews would make a one-off appearance in an episode of the medical drama.

Now in Los Angeles for close to a year, George had amassed a circle of loyal friends. He received the hospitality and assistance of friends such as Thom Matthews gladly. And he was not to forget their support. Many of the friends he made during this lean period remain close friends today.

George's first step towards a career as an actor, involved him enrolling for acting classes. He signed up to study under director/teacher/author/painter, Milton Katselas, who founded Los Angeles acting school, The Beverly Hills Playhouse. The many actors and actresses who have studied under Katselas, himself a one-time acting student under the legendary Lee Strasberg at the Actor's Studio, include Tom Selleck, Michelle Pfeiffer, Ted Danson, Tony Danza, Tyne Daly and Alec Baldwin. Katselas does not teach a specific school of acting – for instance, Method acting – but instead grooms the actor's bag of talent, via a down-to-earth approach. The school emphasizes three aspects of training: acting, administration and attitude. In other words, the school teaches acting, but also trains the actor or actress in the business side of the job.

To fund the course and keep money in his pocket, George worked in construction and as a door-to-door insurance salesman. He has described himself as having been a "horrible insurance salesman." Whether

Below: Milton Katselas, the man whose acting classes George attended, teaching at his school in Beverly Hills.

he liked the work or not, he needed the money. Being so broke was hard, and knowing that he had overridden his father's advice to complete a degree before pursuing acting, he felt under immense pressure to succeed, no matter what.

In reality, these frugal, hungry times taught George a value of money that he has never forgotten. In an interview with Larry King on CNN in 2006, he spoke of his diligence with money: "I do all the things that people who were broke for a long time do, which is you pay cash for everything. You still have this thought in the back of your head that you'll, you know, you'll eventually be broke again so you're always very careful."

Some accounts of George's career report that his first acting job in Los Angeles was in a Panansonic TV commercial. He has never confirmed whether or not this is actually true.

It is, however, a fact that his first real acting break in Los Angeles came when he landed a part in the TV detective series *Riptide*, which starred Perry King, Joe Penny and Murray Bozinsky. George played the role of 'Lenny Colwell' in an

episode called *Where The Girls Are*, which aired on 2 October 1984.

Seeing himself on TV was an exciting first step on the ladder of success but there was also excitement on the personal front. George had met a young actress, Talia Balsam, when the pair worked side by side on a small theatre production. He had taken on several poorly paid theatre parts for experience. It was while working on one such play that he met Talia. He was very much attracted to the actress, but she was already seeing someone. Despite her insistence that she was unavailable, George pursued her relentlessly.

He had recently broken up with actress Judie Aronson, whom he is believed to have dated between 1983-84. Aronson, who was born in Los Angeles on 7 June 1964, was 19 when she started dating George. She first appeared on TV in 1983 in the TV shows *The Powers Of Matthew Star* and *Simon & Simon* and made her film debut in 1984, appearing in the horror

Above left: Talia Balsam and George first met when they were working on a theatre production together, although she was already established in a relationship at the time.

Above right: George began an on-off affair with Talia in 1985 that would lead to marriage four years later.

Above: Talia Balsam's mother, Joyce Van Patten, with Danny Kaye and Harvey Korman.

film, *Friday the 13th: The Final Chapter*.

Talia Balsam was born in New York City on 5 March 1959. Her parents were both in the acting profession. Her father, Martin Balsam, who was born in the Bronx in 1919, had studied acting at the Actor's Studio and, prior to his daughter's birth, had notched up credits in classic films such as *On the Waterfront* and *12 Angry Men*. Her mother, Joyce Van Patten, who was born in New York in 1934, made her acting debut at the age of 14, in an episode of the *Philco Television Playhouse*. She went on to notch up many TV and film roles.

After Talia's birth, both parents continued to accumulate impressive accomplishments. In 1966, her father won the "Best Actor in a Supporting Role" Academy Award for his work in Fred Coe's film, *A Thousand Clowns*. That prestigious win led to parts in classic seventies' films such as *Catch 22*, *Tora Tora Tora* and *Little Big Man*. Joyce went on to pursue a career in TV, appearing in shows like *Dr Kildare*, *The Twilight Zone*, *Perry Mason*, *Hawaii Five-O*, *The Streets Of San Francisco* and *Columbo*. The acting bug wasn't exclusive to her parents. Talia's uncle, Dick Van Patten, and aunt, Patricia Van Patten, were also both actors. It was in her blood to pursue a career in acting, too – just as it was in George's blood to seek a career in the public spotlight.

Talia studied acting at the Treehaven School in Tucson, Arizona and made her acting debut when she was eighteen, appearing in a made-for-TV film called *Alexander: The Other Side of Dawn*. The

film told the story of a teenage boy who heads for Hollywood, dreaming of making it as a movie star. The harsh realities soon smash the dream and he ends up working as a gay prostitute to keep a roof over his head. Talia had a small part in the film, which made its network premiere on 16 May 1977.

The same year, she scored a small part in *Happy Days*, the popular U.S. TV series, which starred Henry Winkler as the Fonz. Playing "Nancy Croft", she appeared across three consecutive episodes. During the rest of the seventies, Talia notched up credits in various made-for-TV films including *The Initiation of Sarah*, *Stickin' Together*, *The Millionaire* (which starred her father), *Survival of Dana* and *Sunnyside*.

In the first years of the eighties, she appeared in TV shows like *Taxi*, *Hill Street Blues*, *Cagney and Lacey* and *Family Ties* – all major vehicles that beamed her into households worldwide.

By the time she met George in 1984, she was appearing in yet further classic U.S. TV shows like *Magnum P.I.* and was in the middle of shooting made-for-TV films such as *Calamity Jane* and *Nadia*. George had comparatively few credits under his belt and was at the very beginning of his career. Redressing that shortfall, George landed a part in a short-lived TV medical drama, called *E/R* – a confusing aspect of George's resumé since he would, of course, later strike it big as Dr Ross in the TV medical drama called *E.R.* But this *E/R* has nothing to do with the later, much celebrated *E.R.*

Above: George shakes hands with Elliot Gould on the set of the TV show *E/R* in 1984.

For George, this was a major break. He was signed up to play "Mark Kolmar" aka "Ace". The show was based on a play called *E/R: Emergency Room* by Ronald Berman, Zaid Farid, Richard Fire, Carolyn-Purdy Gordon, Stuart Gordon, Gary Houston, Tom Towles and Bruce A. Young, which had been produced in early 1982 by the Organic Theater Company of Chicago.

Now reconfigured as a TV show, the lead role of "Dr Howard Sheinfeld" was played by esteemed actor, Elliott Gould. Acting opposite him in the female lead, Mary McDonnell was "Dr Eve Sheridan".

Unlike *E.R.*, this show only lasted one season. The pilot launched the show in September 1984 and the season finale closed it in January 1985. It ran for a total of eighteen half-hour episodes. George appeared in four. The first, "A Cold Night in Chicago", aired on 28 November 1984. The second, "Both Sides Now", aired on 12 December 1984 while the third, "Enter Romance", appeared on 26 December. George's fourth and final appearance, in an episode titled "I Raise You", went out on 23 January 1985.

By then, he had scored a third TV credit, with a one-off appearance in the TV detective show, *Street Hawk*, which starred Rex Smith. He played "Kevin Stark" in an episode called "A Second Self" which aired on 11 January 1985. This meant that American viewers saw George Clooney on their TV sets twice in a twelve-day period, first on *Street Hawk* and then on *E/R*. Whether any noticed the young actor is another story.

Seemingly on a roll, George then landed a part in *Crazy Like A Fox*, a TV series based around the professional tussles of private investigator Harry Fox, Sr. The show, which proved very successful, ran between 1984-86. The episode featuring George, "Suitable For Framing", went out on 31 March 1985.

During this time, the relationship that Talia Balsam had been in when she and George met while working together, had come to an end. In the wings waited a still-enthusiastic George. The pair started dating and for the next eighteen months, they were a couple.

Talia was busy shooting a made-for-TV film. In the gay coming out drama, *Consenting Adult*, she played "Margie". The film gave her an opportunity to act alongside Martin Sheen. During the same period, she also appeared in an episode of the hit TV show, *Murder She Wrote*.

Meanwhile, George's exciting run of work had temporarily come to an end. The rollercoaster nature of the acting profession had whisked him aloft and now dropped him back into the daily grind of auditions. The process of forging a career as an actor was not coming as easily or as quickly as he had hoped.

In May 1985, George turned 24. He was hardly old yet, by the standards of "Brat Pack" actors in demand at the time, such as Rob Lowe and Matt Dillon, he was starting to err on the side of being a late bloomer. He had very nearly become a member of the "Brat Pack" after auditioning for the John Hughes film, *The Breakfast Club*, which opened at U.S. cinemas in February 1985. George made the shortlist of potential actors for the part of bad boy "John Bender", which ended up going to Judd Nelson.

Then came a major break for George. He landed a steady role in the hit TV show, *The Facts of Life*. The show debuted on U.S. TV on 4 May 1979, as a sitcom spin-off

Right: The cast of *The Facts of Life* had been together for six years before George joined them for his first appearance in season seven.
Below: Mindy Cohn shares the sofa with George in *The Facts of Life*.

of *Diff'rent Strokes*. The show centred on "Mrs Garrett" (played by Charlotte Rae), a housemother at an all-girls school. It took a while to acquire a following, but once it caught on, it became enormously successful. The last-ever episode aired on TV on 7 May 1988.

George came into the show during season seven, the only adult male actor in the cast. Introduced as the hunky man in the show, his character first turns up in the second episode of season seven, episode 135, "Into the Frying Pan", which aired on 21 September 1985. His character, "George Burnett", a handsome, thoughtful, builder, is hired by Mrs Garrett and the girls to overhaul Edna's Edibles into Over Our Heads, a shop selling cards, clothes and gifts.

After appearing throughout much of season seven, George made a special guest appearance in season eight, in episode 165, "The Wedding Day", which aired on U.S. TV on 22 November 1986. He also turned up again in episode 168, "Write or Wrong", which went out on 13 December 1986. In episode 172, "A Star Is Torn", airing on 31 January 1987, George Burnett resigned from his job at the store and that was the end of George's involvement with the show.

Around his commitments with *The Facts of Life*, George also found time to squeeze in other appearances in TV shows. He made a one-off appearance in an episode of the TV show, *Hotel*, which starred James Brolin. He appeared in an episode called "Recriminations", playing "Nick Miller", which aired on 29 January 1986. Later that year, he appeared as "Rollo Moldonado", in an episode of the TV show, *Throb*, called "My Fair Punker Lady". Starring Maryedith Burrell and Don Calfa, the show revolved around thirtysomething single mother divorcée, "Sandy Beatty" (played by Diana Canova), who takes a job working for a small, new-wave record label. The episode with George aired on 21 October 1986.

Meanwhile, George had also scored his

first proper role in a feature-length film. The part was that of "Major Biff Woods" in Neal Israel's made-for-TV film, *Combat High*. At the time, Israel was known as the director of frat boy comedy, *Bachelor Party*, which starred the young Tom Hanks and reached cinemas in June 1984.

This new film by the then 30-year-old Israel was a comedy, set in a military academy (think *Taps* meets *Police Academy*). It starred Keith Gordon and Wallace Langham, as two hard-to-control high school students sent to the academy for some boot camp discipline. Written by Paul W. Shapiro, the film was shot on location in Missouri, primarily at the real-life Kemper Military School in Boonville, Missouri. The film made its TV premiere on NBC on 23 November 1986.

Technically speaking, this was not George's film acting debut. He had, of course, earlier appeared in *And They're Off*, which was never released. And he had appeared in a 1984 film called *Predator: the Concert* (aka *Grizzly II: the Concert*). The film, starring Steve Innwood, told the story of a grizzly bear terrorising an outdoor rock 'n' roll concert. Shot on location in Hungary during 1983, the film was not released until 1987 – hence its status as George's official movie debut, even if the delayed release date suggests otherwise. The film was the sequel to 1976 horror film, *Grizzly*. Other future talents, Charlie Sheen and Laura Dern,

Above: In *The Facts of Life*, George played hunky builder "George Burnett".

Left: While appearing in *The Facts of Life*, George also landed parts in the TV series *Hotel* and *Throb* as well as his first film role in *Combat High*.

Above: Anthony Starke with George in the 1988 movie *Return of the Killer Tomatoes.*

appeared alongside the young George in the forgettable film.

In the latter half of 1986, George got stuck into another film part, this time playing "Oliver" in Bill Froehlich's directorial debut, *Return To Horror High*. The story was straightforward – a film crew return to an abandoned school where a serial killer had once run rampage attacking students. Predictably, when they start recreating and filming a dramatised account of the true story, members of the crew and cast start disappearing one by one, suggesting that the serial killer is not only still on the loose but up to his old tricks. The horror film was released to cinemas in the U.S. on 28 January 1987. The film took roughly $200,000 over its opening weekend and ended up grossing just over $1 million in the U.S., not exactly the kind of takings that would attach George's name to a box office success or give his agent any juicy leverage.

Meanwhile, the TV roles continued. First up, a guesting role in TV cop drama, *Hunter*, which starred Fred Dryer as Detective Sgt Rick Hunter. George appeared as "Matthew Winfield", in an episode titled "Double Exposure", which aired on 14 February 1987. A month later, on 15 March, he played "Kip Howard"

in an episode of the TV show, *Murder She Wrote*, called "No Laughing Murder". And in May, George made an appearance in silver-haired hit sitcom, *The Golden Girls*, playing "Bobby Hopkins" in an episode called "To Catch A Neighbour." That summer, he also played a drug dealer in a play called *Vicious*, staged at the Steppenwolf Theatre in Chicago.

Talia was also incredibly busy. During 1987, she played "Sharon Raymond" in a horror film, *The Kindred*, alongside Rod Steiger. She also appeared in an episode of the TV show, *Tales From The Darkside* and took on other parts in made-for-TV films. She played "Jenny Fox" in *P.I. Private Investigations*, "Linda" in *The Ladies* and "Judy Cusimano" in *In The Mood* (starring opposite a young Patrick Dempsey, later a star on TV show *Grey's Anatomy*). Like George, she was constantly working during 1986-87. Neither has specified whether their combined hectic work schedules put a strain on the relationship but, late in 1987, their eighteen-month romance came to an end.

Next up for George was a part in *Bennett Brothers*, a thirty-minute pilot episode for a new NBC sitcom about mismatched, polar opposite brothers sharing an apartment. It would be the first of many TV pilots that

George would work on, only for the show never to go any further.

Bennett Brothers pitted George as "Tom Bennett" against his brother "Richard Bennett", played by Richard Kind. George and Richard Kind hit it off from the first day they met and became very close friends. Several years later, when George would find himself in a time of personal turmoil and crisis, Richard Kind would be the one to provide tremendous support and a place to stay.

The pilot was written by Lloyd Garver and directed by Will MacKenzie, who at the time had directorial credits to his name on shows such as *WRKP In Cincinnati*, *Moonlighting*, *Remington Steele* and *Family Ties*. The pilot, once in the can, was ill-fated and NBC never aired it on television.

George was then offered a part in a film called *Return Of the Killer Tomatoes!* The film, which received a limited release in the summer of 1988, was directed by John De Bello. It was a sequel to the director's earlier 1978 film, *Attack of the Killer Tomatoes*. In both cases, plotlines follow b-movie formulas and revolve around tomatoes turning against the human race. With typical self-deprecatory humour, George reflected back on the role in an interview with *The Chicago Sun Times* in 2002, saying: "I still made $100,000 that year and that's a great living, even if you're being attacked by large vegetables."

George cannot have taken the role of "Matt Stevens" with any doubt in his mind that this was anything but a way to pay the rent. His goal was to keep working as

Above: Down on the beach, George is involved in a heated debate over whether a tomato should be regarded as a vegetable or a fruit.

an actor. And whether the projects were of artistic merit or not, he signed on the dotted line. His father had instilled in him a feverish work ethic. A few years after this career low, George told *TV Guide* that he had always made it a policy to take on as many acting jobs as possible, in a bid to build up his career. "I've always had a fairly good eye for what I was doing: 'Hey it's a piece of fluff but I'm going to make some nice money.' Or 'Oh, man, I've done something special.'"

No longer with Talia Balsam, George started dating 26-year-old model turned actress, Kelly Preston. At the time, she was best known for appearing in the film *Christine*, an adaptation of the Stephen King novel. The pair met at a party thrown by their shared talent agency and quickly fell for each other. She was born Kelly Kamalelehua Palzis in Honolulu on 13 October 1962. After modelling as a teen, she studied acting at the Beverly Hills Playhouse and then studied drama at the University of Southern California. In 1983, she changed her name to Kelly Preston. In 1985, she married actor Kevin Gage. They separated in 1988. She met George soon after with George having recently broken up with Talia Balsam – not that he and Talia were done quite yet.

George was rescued from further b-movie parts, when he landed a major mainstream recurring part in ABC's soon-to-launch TV show, *Roseanne*. The working class family sitcom starred Roseanne Barr and John Goodman. In some ways, George's new part was a continuation of the role of "George Burnett" on *The Facts of Life* – that of a handsome blue collar worker – and his success in that show must have set him up nicely to land this next part of "Booker Brooks". The part required that he play the overbearing boss at the plastics factory where Roseanne and her sister, "Jackie", worked. As he entered the show, the plotline stipulated that Booker, a bit of a hunk in the workplace, had at one point dated Jackie.

George first appeared in the pilot episode of the show, titled "Life And Stuff", which premiered on 18 October 1988. From there on, George would make intermittent appearances across eleven episodes, the last of which, "Trick Me Up, Trick Me Down" aired on 29 October 1991.

The show became massively successful. During its first season, it was the second most watched TV show in the U.S. With that success, George became a minor household name. Viewers liked the love interest between Booker and Jackie – and the sparring between Booker and Roseanne.

Meanwhile, George and Kelly Preston were reported to have bought a home together in the Hollywood Hills. She gave him a gift – a Vietnamese potbellied pig called Max whom George loved from the moment he set eyes on him. By all accounts, George and Kelly enjoyed a quiet life when not working. He spent his spare time building furniture and collecting old cars. The relationship, which had hurried into being, fizzled out just as quickly.

In mid-1989, he and Kelly separated. In the state of mind to ring the changes, George then made moves to leave *Roseanne*. He later told *TV Guide* that he felt like he was playing "seventh banana on the number one show."

Above: George's seemingly blissful relationship with Kelly Preston was to be short-lived.
Left: Kelly and George bought a home together in the Hollywood Hills and she gave him the Vietnamese potbellied pig called Max who was to be his companion for the next eighteen years.

His ambition was too restless. He was 28 years old and he did not want to turn thirty without being close to a shot at top billing.

He shared his concerns with his parents. His father told him he was against his son's plans to leave the hit show, especially since *Roseanne* had offered George a substantial sum of money to stay on as Booker. *Time* magazine quoted Nick Clooney as saying, "I was thinking he could build a little nest egg and maybe acting would pay off after all. He said, 'No, I'll be in a cul-de-sac. I'll be that guy, and that's all I'll be.'" And that was that, George quit *Roseanne*. His last appearance was in an episode that aired 2 May 1989.

Meanwhile, George was not single for long. In the wake of his split from Kelly Preston, he got back in touch with Talia Balsam. Soon, they were dating again. Talia had had a quiet 1988, appearing in a made-for-TV film, *Tales from the Hollywood Hills* and guest appearing in the TV show, *Tour of Duty*. When she and George got back together, she had just finished shooting a made-for-TV film called *Trust Me*. She was gearing up for a guest appearance in hit U.S. TV show, *Thirtysomething*, which would air in December 1989.

This time, George did not take things slowly. He proposed and she accepted. They acted fast and headed to Las Vegas in his Winnebago. There, surrounded by friends, they were married in a chapel by an Elvis Presley impersonator on 15 December 1989. George later said of the wedding, "When you come from Kentucky, any kind of white trash thing like that impresses you." As soon as they had exchanged vows, on came the drinking and gambling. "I had already done the big gamble," George later reflected in an interview with *TV Guide*. "I figured: how much more could I lose?"

The 1980s came to an end with George, 28 years old, suddenly married and freshly out of his contract with hit TV show, *Roseanne*. He was sure the world was now his oyster and set his sights on the big time.

Left: George as "Booker Brooks" with John Goodman and Roseanne Barr in *Roseanne*.

3

OUT OF SIGHT

A successful run as "seventh banana" on the number one U.S. TV show did not, however, guarantee George the pick of the best roles out there. Frustratingly, he found himself back on the audition circuit. He ended up waiting longer than he might have expected for his next part. It came in the guise of a new TV sitcom about a group of friends called *Knights of the Kitchen Table*. The show was produced by UBU productions, the company behind *Family Ties* and *Spin City*. A pilot was shot in 1990, with George starring opposite Jessica Steen. George played "Rick", Jessica played "Marla". In the pilot, Marla comes out as a lesbian.

If the show had made it past pilot stage, this would have made her one of the first overtly lesbian characters on primetime U.S. television. But it wasn't to be. The pilot was never aired on TV and the show died a death. Stills from the pilot, available to view on the internet, show George clad in a black leather jacket and sporting long, shoulder length hair – a far cry from the trademark Caesar cut that George is known for today.

George's next role was in *Red Surf*, a 1990 film directed by H. Gordon Boos. The film stars George as "Remar" opposite Doug Savant (best known these days as "Tom" on *Desperate Housewives*) as "Attila". The pair are hard-living surfers and casual drug dealers who get themselves into a bind when they become involved with a major drug cartel. In the female lead is Dedee Pfeiffer, sister of Michelle Pfeiffer, whom George is believed to have briefly dated back in 1985 when Talia Balsam was "unavailable". She plays "Rebecca", Remar's girlfriend. The film also featured a cameo by rock star

Gene Simmons, of KISS fame. The film grossed $13,136 at the U.S. box office – a shockingly low take.

Then it was time for another pilot for a TV show. This one, a cop drama for ABC, had the working title of *Sunset Beat*. George was signed up to play "Chic Chesbro", opposite Michael DeLuise as "Tim Kelly". They were part of a division of Los Angeles cops who went undercover as bikers in order to bust street crime in an American town. The storyline was not dissimilar to *21 Jump Street*, the cop vehicle which catapulted Johnny Depp to fame. The sixty-minute pilot aired on 21 April 1990, followed by a second episode, a week later, on 28 April. The show was then axed by ABC.

Next, keeping up a furious work pace, George signed up to appear in a new ABC show called *Baby Talk*. The show was inspired by the film, *Look Who's Talking* and revolved around a single mother, "Maggie" (Julia Duffy) and her son, "Mickey". George had a starring role as "Joe", a construction worker – and played him with a shock of thick dark hair.

In July 1990, George's uncle George Guilfoyle, after whom he had been named, was on his deathbed, terminally ill with cancer. George went out to Philadelphia to be by his bedside.

That summer, he was busy shooting *Baby Talk*. When he came back to Los Angeles, after being with his uncle, he was thinking differently. His uncle was only 65. His death warned George, who was now 29, on the precipice of turning thirty, that life was fleeting. He resolved to go all the way with his acting, striving to achieve excellence.

He elaborated later on how he was feeling when his uncle died, in an interview with *USA Weekend*, "As he was dying, I held his hand. He kept saying, What a waste, because he was a 65-year-old guy who had so much promise and didn't do anything with it. I thought, the only thing I won't allow myself to do is wake up at 65 and go, 'What a waste.' If I get hit by a bus now, everybody will go,

Previous spread:
George astride
a motorcycle as
"Chic Chesbro" in
Sunset Beat.
Right: George with
Connie Selleca in
Baby Talk, the show
he walked out on.
Far Right: The
undercover cop show
Sunset Beat lasted for
only two episodes.

'Well, he jammed a lot in.'"

This new zest for work led him to various clashes with the powerful executive producer on *Baby Talk*, Ed Weinberger. Eventually, the static came to a head, as George told *TV Guide*, "We had several infamous fights. At some point I said: 'You know what, you can't pay me enough to be treated like this.' So I stood up for myself."

And with that, he announced he was quitting. In response, Weinberger explained to George the potential repercussions of such a move. George went home, worried he would be blacklisted from Hollywood. "I was a hothead at that point," he later reflected. "I just said, 'No more!' I thought I had ended my career. I thought it was over."

He needn't have worried.

Four days after he quit *Baby Talk*, he was offered another role in a pilot show – *Rewrite For Murder*, which CBS were developing. The one-hour pilot saw George playing "Nick Biano" opposite Beth Broderick and Pam Dawbey. As before, the pilot was a one-off and CBS decided not to take the show any further.

Meanwhile, Talia had appeared in a second episode of *Thirtysomething* and a second episode of *Murder She Wrote*. She was also acting in a slew of films. The first, an independent comic short film called *The Walter Ego*, saw her play a character somewhat unenticingly called "Susie The Whore". Next, she played "Emma" in a legal thriller called *Killer Instinct*. Then "Liz" in a made-for-TV film, *Sins Of the Mother*. On top of that, she also appeared in episodes of three TV shows – *Life Goes On*, *Stat* and *Jake and the Fatman*.

Finally, *Baby Talk* premiered on TV on 8 March 1991. On account of having quit the show, George only appeared in a scattering of episodes. The pilot episode; the episode going out a week later on 15 March; the fourth episode which screened on 29 March and lastly, episode twelve in that first season, which aired on 17 May 1991.

On 6 May 1991, George turned thirty. He took stock of his career. Although

he had achieved mainstream attention for his work in *The Facts of Life* and *Roseanne*, he was still frustrated at how hard it was to break into credible feature film acting. He kept going for auditions and not getting the parts. He read no less than five times for Ridley Scott's *Thelma and Louise*, auditioning for the part of "J.D", which ended up going to Brad Pitt. He later said, "I remember when he got it. I didn't know who he was. I was like, 'Fuck that guy.' I knew it was a great part." Later, of course, they were to act side-by-side and become firm friends.

While his film career failed to leave the starting blocks, his TV career, since leaving Roseanne, had been cursed with a staccato series of false starts. Too many abandoned TV shows were piling up. He felt the pressure of the milestone. He was also feeling under pressure at home, as he and Talia began to experience problems in their marriage.

On 14 September 1991, *Rewrite For Murder* premiered on CBS. It was to be the first and last screening of the show. A month later, more positively, George made a special guest appearance in season four of *Roseanne*. The episode, "Trick Me Up, Trick Me Down", aired on 29 October and saw George once more step into the role of the hectoring Booker Brooks. After his checkered resume since leaving the hit TV show, he must have

"EVEN WHEN
THINGS
WEREN'T
GREAT AND I
WAS DOING
SUNSET BEAT
OR *BABY TALK*
ON TV, I STILL
FELT LIKE A
WINNER."

wondered at times if he had made the
right decision in abandoning *Roseanne*.

Much of 1992 was taken up by a new
TV role for George – that of "Detective
Ryan Walker" in a cop series called *Bodies
of Evidence*. The show premiered on
18 June 1992. The first season featured
eight episodes, each lasting one hour and
wrapped on 27 August. George appeared
across all eight episodes, acting alongside
"Lieutenant Ben Carroll" (played by Lee
Horsley), "Detective Nora Houghton"
(played by Kate McNeil) and "Detective
Will Stratton" (played by Al Fann).
George wore his hair short and came
across as a smooth individual. The show
was a fairly straightforward cop drama,
with each episode seeing the detectives
assigned to a difficult case. The regularity
of the role was good for George. He spoke
later of such continuity of employment in
TV, "You don't struggle if you're a regular
on a TV series. You make a lot of money."

All the while, he kept telling himself
that he was succeeding – simply because
he was sustaining a career as an actor,
year in, year out. He knew some jobs
were for the money and that others had
integrity. He elaborated on this in an
interview with *The Chicago Sun Times*,
saying, "Even when things weren't great
and I was doing *Sunset Beat* or *Baby Talk*
on TV, I still felt like a winner. I knew

Right: George had
a new short haircut
and a new smooth
image for his role
as "Detective Ryan
Walker" in *Bodies of
Evidence*.

Far Right: George was
to play yet another
detective in the TV
series *Sisters*.

they were terrible shows, but I had a job."

Alongside *Bodies Of Evidence*, George
found time to play "Mac" in a comic film
called *Unbecoming Age* (also sometimes
referred to as *Magic Bubble*). The
storyline follows a woman's change of
life after despairing at turning forty. It's
a riff on a typical elixir of youth fantasy.
George's character crosses paths with
the suburban housewife, "Julia" (Diane
Salinger) at a supermarket and falls in
love with her. The film was the first and
last that Alfredo and Deborah Ringel
co-directed. Although the film screened
at the Los Angeles film festival in July
1992, it doesn't appear to have ever
received a theatrical release. A decade
later, however, when George had become
famous, it was released on DVD.

Moving into 1993, George appeared in
Alan J. Levi's *Without Warning: Terror in
the Towers*, a made-for-TV film. The film
was based on the events of February 1993,
when terrorists attacked the World Trade
Center, by detonating a car bomb in a car
park beneath the buildings. This film was
rushed into production soon after the
attack. Starring James Avery, it aired on 26
May 1993 – only three months after the
terrorist attack. George played "Kevin Shea".

While George was shooting the film,
the second and final season of *Bodies
of Evidence* was on TV screens in the
U.S. As with the first season, there were
eight sixty-minute episodes, running
from 30 March 1993 until 28 May 1993.
While both roles gave George continued
mainstream exposure and a decent pay
cheque, neither brought him the kind of
acclaim he so desperately wanted.

As George spent 1992 playing
Detective Ryan Walker, Talia was going
through a lean patch. After appearing in
Jake and The Fatman in 1991, she is not
credited again until she appeared in an
episode of *The Larry Sanders Show* which
went out during August 1993.

The explanation would seem to lie
in the breakdown of her marriage to
George. By late 1992, they were already

> "I'VE BECOME VERY AWARE OF GETTING DEEPLY INVOLVED WITH WOMEN. I'M PROBABLY PUTTING UP A DEFENSIVE SHIELD BECAUSE I DON'T WANT TO GO THROUGH A HEAVY BREAK-UP."

in the throes of a divorce. George had moved out of their house in Los Angeles and in with his friend, Richard Kind, whom he had met while shooting the *Bennett Brothers* pilot. George has said of this era that he was "stone broke" and lived in Kind's spare bedroom for nine months. He has also said that another of his close friends, Grant Heslov, an actor, would "take me to dinner and pay for everything. He took care of me." He was stressed and reportedly suffered terrible health on account of a stomach ulcer. Plagued by pain and weight gain, George consulted a herbalist and three months of treatment later, the ulcer which had plagued George for two years, was healed.

Talia's next credit for the period is an appearance in *Mad About You*, the TV show, in October 1993. By then, her marriage to George was legally over. As to why the marriage crumbled, Talia is quoted as saying, "George spent more time with his friends than me during our marriage." She is, of course, referring to 'the Boys', George's legendary inner circle of male friends. Apparently, starting as a tradition in 1988, George and the boys meet at his house every Sunday morning. They go riding, head to Malibu, and play basketball. Then they take a jacuzzi and steam. Later they tend to barbecue. When one of them is in trouble, they all rally round.

By September 1993, their divorce was finalised. It had cost George dearly, both emotionally and financially. He has said that he spent $80,000 on legal fees alone, never mind the actual undisclosed settlement. He returned to being single, openly stating that he would not marry again. He later told *The Sunday Mirror*, "I also went through hell in my marriage a while back and that wasn't pleasant

either. So I've become wary of getting deeply involved with women. I'm probably putting up a defensive shield because I don't want to go through a heavy break-up."

George has said what he thinks went wrong with their marriage, "Talia and I were together for a long time. She was the girl I chased and was in love with, the girl I always wanted to marry. I was 28 and in Kentucky when you get to be that age, you're supposed to get married and you know exactly what the marriage should be like. I had this image of marriage. When ours didn't exactly fit that image, I thought it didn't work. I wasn't very bright about it. We had to reconstruct our marriage a little bit and I wasn't willing to do that. I walked away. I could have been scared. Maybe I wasn't ready to be married. It was my fault all down the line."

The only distraction during this painful period was work. He was offered another TV show – this one called *The Building*. He shot the pilot, appearing as the former fiancée of the central character, "Bonnie", a young woman living in Chicago (played by Bonnie Hunt). The show's storyline revolved around the characters who also lived in Bonnie's apartment building. Once more the pilot premiered on 20 August 1993, only for the show to be dropped thereafter.

To keep his morale up, George introduced himself as a "film actor", not a TV actor. It was the power of positive thinking. Many would have bailed out by this point. Not George. He kept pushing on, telling himself how close he was to that one giant break that would open all the doors. "I always used to say: I'm a film actor, despite the fact that I'd hardly been in any movies. I reasoned to myself, I just happen to be doing television. It kept me going."

Next George landed a solid, long-term role in the TV drama, *Sisters*. The show was already established and had been on air since 1991. It told the everyday life stories of a group of sisters: "Teddy" (Sela Ward), "Alex" (Swoosie Kurtz), "Georgie" (Patricia Kalember), "Frankie" (Julianne Phillips) and "Charley" (Jo Anderson & Sheila Kelley).

Previous spread: Mark Frankel, Sela Ward and George in the *Sisters* episode "The Things We Do For Love."
Right: TV viewers loved the on-screen chemistry between George and Sela Ward in *Sisters*.

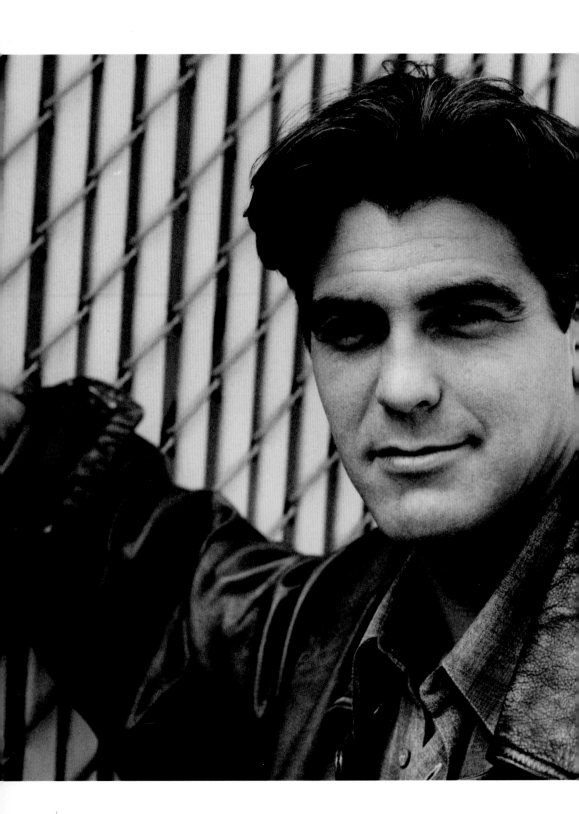

George was brought in to play "Detective James Falconer". His character's connection to the lives of the sisters was through Teddy. The two damaged souls meet, get closer, tiptoe towards a relationship, get engaged, then marry. Throughout the span of their relationship, viewers loved the onscreen chemistry between George and Sela Ward – mirroring later interest in the onscreen romance between "Dr Ross" and "Carol Hathaway" on *E.R.*

The show would eventually run for six seasons, ending in May 1996. George was involved with the show across 19 episodes, spanning a year. The first went on air on 2 October 1993. The last went on air on 18 October 1994. George's role in the show ended when Falconer was murdered. His death devastates Teddy completely and the trauma induces psychosomatic blindness.

Also in 1993, George found time to drop down to Mexico, to shoot a tiny part in a film called *The Harvest*. Written and directed by David Marconi, it starred his cousin Miguel Ferrer, as a screenwriter who takes a break at a Mexican beach resort, only to find himself immersed in a body organ smuggling ring. Being on set with Miguel must have been a nostalgic experience for George, taking him back to 1981 and stepping onto the set of *And They're Off* in Kentucky – that fateful encounter with acting which determined his future.

In this film, George famously appears as a character listed as "lip syncing transvestite". The part required George to don drag and lip sync to Berlinda Carlisle's "Heaven On Earth". In a wig comprised of blonde curly locks, a black leather jacket and a gold bra and skirt, it was a far cry from Detective James Falconer's smouldering masculinity. The film opened as a limited release at U.S. cinemas on 5 November 1993. Considering the part today, which sits as one of several lows on George's resumé, you realise that when he agreed to appear in the film, George must have genuinely had no idea that within the year he would be a household name.

Left: George's participation in *Sisters* ended when his character, "Detective James Falconer" was murdered.

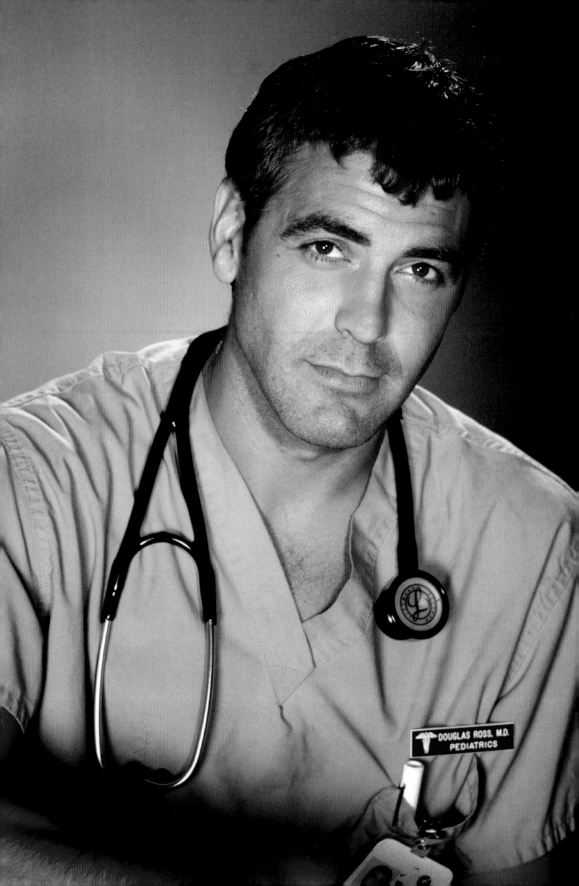

4

THE *E.R.* YEARS

And then George felt the need to get away. Yes, his ulcer had cleared
up. Yes, the steady TV work was paying a decent wage. But he was still
wrung out after the divorce. To clear his head, he decided to set out
on a road trip with his close friend, Grant Heslov – one of the boys.
They packed up George's Winnebago and hit the road. George was also
waiting to hear about a TV part. Before setting out on the road trip, he
had appeared in the pilot for a new medical drama called *E.R.* (short for
Emergency Room). He had heard about the pilot script while shooting
episodes of *Sisters* and made a point of getting his hands on a copy.
The status of the show depended on whether a network picked it up.

The show was set in the fictional Chicago County General hospital and focused on stories associated both with patients seeking emergency medical treatment and hospital staff. This meant viewers would be involved episode-to-episode in the everyday lives of the doctors, nurses and hospital management, as well as constantly changing dramatic stories arising from cases presenting at the E.R. The action would be fast and authentic and the characterisation would be vivid and personal. The show was the brainchild of novelist Michael Crichton and produced by R. Scott Gemmill, John Wells, David Zabel and Christopher Chulack.

Crichton was born in 1942 and graduated from Harvard Medical School in 1969. He paid his way through medical school by writing thrillers under a pseudonym. During his final year studying medicine, he wrote and sold a medical thriller called *The Andromeda Strain*. The novel was a huge success and film rights were sold to Hollywood. He then wrote a non-fiction book titled *Five Patients: Hospital Explained*, published in 1970. After graduating, he worked briefly as a postdoctoral fellow at the Jonas Salk Institute for Biological Science in La Jolla, California, before leaving to write full time. Many successful books have followed. Back in 1974, he had written a screenplay called *E.R.*, which drew heavily on his own personal experiences. While discussing his 1990 novel *Jurassic Park* with Steven Spielberg, which the pair transformed into one of the highest grossing films of all time, he mentioned the old screenplay, long dormant, and Spielberg expressed interest. Crichton was reluctant to blow dust off the old work but was eventually won over by Spielberg's enthusiasm. The latter's production company, Amblin Entertainment, revisited Crichton's old screenplay and reconceived it for TV.

Once Warner Bros were on board as backers for the two-hour pilot episode, the cast could be hired.

It was somewhat fated – George had already notched up a credit appearing in *E/R* – the earlier medical drama. He therefore had some experience working on a hospital drama and was *au fait* with the medical terminology that would be part and parcel of working on this new show, *E.R.* He had also just come off working on *Sisters* – another show backed by Warner Bros. Once he got hold of the script, he auditioned for executive producer, John Wells and convinced him that he was perfect for the part of "Dr Doug Ross", a hard-drinking, womanising, good-looking paediatrician with a big, big heart. George told Wells he liked "the flaws" in Dr Ross' character.

Now, out on the road with Heslov, he was anxiously waiting to hear the fate of the pilot. With his history of shooting pilots that never materialised into TV shows, he had every right to believe that this pilot would also fail to get off the ground.

E.R. had some challenging elements. There were no star actors or actresses, so to speak. The storylines were mostly dark, consumed with life's difficulties and bleak realities. Nobody knew if a network would pick up such a gritty, realistic show. Plus, each one-hour episode was slated to have multiple storylines running in tandem – which some viewers may have struggled to keep up with.

Consequently, the road trip was kicked into play to take his mind off the stress of waiting to hear, and to celebrate life settling down after the recent turmoil of the divorce. *Sisters* was still showing on TV, featuring his character, but it would be coming to an end that Autumn. Heslov, in turn, was getting over breaking up with his fiancée. Of the road trip, George has said, "We'd stop at each state line on the freeway and tee up a golf ball into the next state. It was just an idea. You know, let's go state-to-state, playing

Right: As "Dr Doug Ross" Clooney played the part of a hard-drinking, womanizing paediatrician with a big heart.

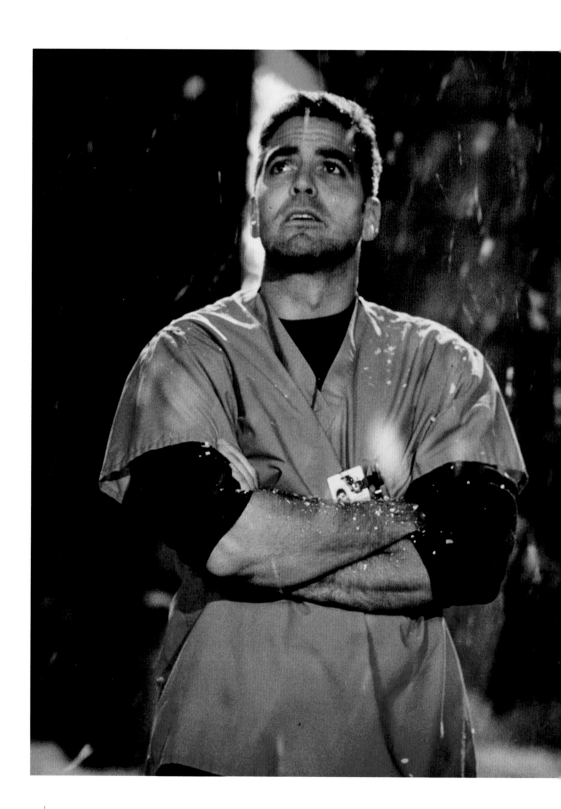

through the problem, so to speak."

Midway through the trip, as they were driving through Arizona, George's cell phone suddenly rang. It was his agent calling to tell him that *E.R.* had been picked up by NBC. Famously, he came off the phone call, turned to Heslov and said, "I just got a career."

George was in. He was signed up to a five-season contract, with a paycheque of $42,000 per episode. His fellow co-stars were Anthony Edwards (as "Dr Mark Greene"), Eriq La Salle (as "Dr Peter Benton"), Noah Wyle (as "Dr John Carter"), Sherry Stringfield (as "Dr Susan Lewis") and Julianna Margulies (as "Nurse Carol Hathaway").

George threw himself into preparing for the role of Dr Doug Ross, feeling excited at where he could take the character. Coming out of a patch in his life where he'd been knocked around, he felt a kinship with Ross's world weary persona. He also felt he'd been around the block enough times to know what he felt was right and wrong, and this helped him, as an actor, to get inside the head of Ross when he boiled over every time an injustice cropped up at the hospital.

The first episode premiered on NBC on 19 September 1994. The launch night – a Monday – had everybody involved in the show feeling worried. The same evening, there was a major sports event – an NFL game which saw Dallas and Detroit go head-to-head in a gripping contest. Despite this potential distraction, when viewing figures came in the following day, it turned out that almost 18 million American households had tuned in, pronouncing the show an instant success.

George was suddenly on the crest of a wave. Everything was changing. Aged 33, it was all coming together. Three episodes of *Sisters* were still to run across late September/October. After that, he was signed to *E.R.* for the forseeable future. Finally, he was affiliated with a TV show that was going to be massive.

Instead of kicking back and enjoying life as a potential TV star, he immediately re-focussed his ambition. He had been in TV too long to count on stability, even if he knew that 18 million viewers spelled a hit show in the making. He had also seen how TV shows typecast actors and actresses, rendering them inseparable in the public's imagination from the

Left: George signed up for five seasons of *E.R.* at $42,000 per episode.
Above: George's original co-stars in the series, Eriq La Salle, Julianna Margulies, Anthony Edwards, Sherry Stringfield and Noah Wyle.

characters they play. He didn't want to be branded as Dr Ross for the rest of his life. He'd already played his fair share of blue collar characters after early success in *The Facts of Life* and thereafter more than his fair share of detectives, following his shield-carrying on screen debut as Chic Chesbro in *Sunset Beat*. Out of that awareness of how the TV business worked, George began wracking his brain to find a way to break into Hollywood and land a credible feature film role.

That first episode of *E.R.* lived up to the hype. The frenzied, high-adrenaline pace hooked viewers from the outset. The breathless storylines, realistic acting, authentic setting, hyperactive camerawork and intriguing behind-the-façade insights into the real life of an *E.R.* unit, proved a winning formula.

In that pilot episode, the leading characters were literally hurled into viewers' living rooms. Chief Resident, Dr Mark Greene, is ready to throw in the towel and quit working at the fictional county hospital. He's considering moving over into private practice, where he can get a juicier paycheque. Into his career dilemma, enter a barrage of patients with all manner of emergency ailments that require life-saving medical treatment.

Unlike other medical dramas such as *Chicago Hope*, *E.R.* succeeded in suspending disbelief and genuinely making viewers feel as though every patient who was rushed through the doors to the E.R. might die. Into Dr Greene's fold, comes Dr John Carter, a sensitive, trust funder, third-year medical student. He is assigned to Dr Peter Benton, a no-nonsense terrific surgeon in the making.

Then George makes his first appearance as Dr Ross, a smooth, slightly stubbled, smoky-voiced, drawling paediatrician. Topping the dramatic mix, Nurse Carol Hathaway is gurneyed into the E.R. after a suicide attempt. Viewers quickly realise that Carol works in the E.R and that her despair has arisen from a failed dalliance with Dr Ross.

That Thursday, 22 September, the same week the pilot went out, the series premiere aired in what would become the regular *E.R.* slot of 10-11 p.m. Again, the viewing figures were outstanding, as repeat and new viewers tuned in to see the next instalment. Against a backdrop of Dr Carter realising just how crazy the E.R. can be, Dr Ross goes to see Carol, who is recuperating from her suicide attempt.

It was later explained that Julianna Margulies' character was only meant to be in the show for the pilot and that in the script, Carol Hathaway dies. But in test screenings, audiences loved Carol's character and the potential storyline between her and Dr Ross. As a result, her character was written back to life and more thickly into the plot.

Over the coming weeks, viewers got used to Dr Ross – his fondness for drinking, his habitual flirting with women, his on/off romantic dance with Nurse Hathaway, his commitment phobia and the maverick intensity of his moral compass. With each episode, he stepped ever closer to centre stage as

Right: The on-screen relationship between Julianna Margulies and George became one of the talking points of the show right from the first episode.
Far Right: When *E.R.* became an international success, George refused to renegotiate his fee, despite the fact that others, such as Anthony Andrews, were reported to be earning eight times as much as him per episode.

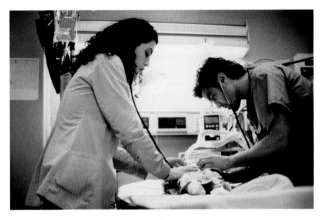

almost 35 million viewers were tuning in for each episode, nearly double the audience for the pilot.

That month, George was put on the cover of *TV Guide* magazine, a portrait shot running under the headline 'ER's George Clooney sets pulses racing as TV's Hot doc'. Inside, a major profile assessed his "drop dead good looks, roguish appeal and teddy bear charm", noting that his was no overnight success story and instead one of a long, hard slog across twelve years of TV and film work. During the article, his looks and growing female following, were played up, as the reporter used phrases like "hunk du jour" and "sexy paediatrician" to contextualise his success and explain the large mailbag from adoring female fans which was thudding onto the doormat at NBC's offices every morning. It also dubbed him as the "Tom Selleck of NBC's smash hit E.R.", though perhaps it might have been more apt to have compared him to Cary Grant, Harrison Ford or Sean Connery.

The cover chimed with a guest appearance on another hit TV show – *Friends*. George appeared in the episode "The One With Two Parts: 2" which went out on 23 February 1995. He and fellow *E.R.* star Noah Wyle appeared together – as doctors. George played "Dr Michael Mitchell". They were worked into a storyline in which "Rachel" sprains her ankle when taking down the Christmas lights lingering on the balcony. She and "Monica" head for hospital, where they are treated by George and Noah, playfully alluding to their work on fellow NBC show *E.R.*

The episode of *E.R.*, "Motherhood", which first aired on 5 May 1995, was guest directed by none other than Quentin Tarantino, then riding high after the success of *Reservoir Dogs* and *Pulp Fiction*. There was a lot of hype in the weeks leading up to the episode airing, with TV critics and audiences (and the hip cinema crowd) wondering what Tarantino would do with the show's

the show's flawed hero. Ross was never afraid to risk his career and reputation by breaking rules if he thought they needed to be broken in the name of doing the right thing, whether that meant protecting a pregnant teenager's necessary confidentiality, punching out an abusive father or procuring drugs for an asthmatic girl whose mother has no way of affording them.

E.R. set Dr Ross up as a handsome, heart-on-sleeve do-gooder and then offset the nice guy streak by also lending him darker, edgier womanising and drinking tendencies. He was both good guy supreme and bad boy supreme, in the same package. His erratic mood swings created an irresistible mix for viewers. Was it an episode where he'd be saving a child in need or giving Carol the mischievous runaround?

Week to week, the show's swelling fan base waited with baited breath to see if he and Carol would get it together. But beyond a tantalising kiss, it didn't happen. Not in series one anyway. Dr Ross got into a relationship with a divorcée with a young son. And Carol was seeing an older lover, "Tag", who wanted her to move in with him. The two came close to a relationship when they grew over-attached to a six-year-old Russian girl with AIDS, "Tatiana", a storyline that emerged in the episode that went out on 9 February 1995. By then,

format. The arrival of Tarantino on set proved interesting. He and George had already crossed paths when George read for the part of "Mr Blonde" when the director was casting for *Reservoir Dogs*. The reading didn't go well and the part ended up going to Michael Madsen. Now, it seemed like fate. Tarantino and George bonded while shooting the episode of *E.R.* Before too long, they'd be working together again. But for now, it was all about a storyline in which Susan's wayward sister, "Chloe", gives birth and Dr Ross is thrown by his girlfriend "Diane" announcing that she thinks it might be a good idea if they move in together.

The season finale came on 18 May 1995, with Doug Ross still weighing up that proposal from Diane and his eyes on Carol Hathaway. Fans didn't have to wait long for the second series – which would launch on 21 September 1995.

In the meantime, the summer gave George time to fulfil a dream: appear in that credible feature film. The film was *From Dusk Till Dawn*, directed by Roberto Rodriguez, whose previous credits included *El Mariachi* and *Desperado* (starring Antonio Banderas and Salma Hayek). The screenplay, adapted from a story by Robert Kurtzman, was by Quentin Tarantino, who was also slated to act in the film. George won the part of "Seth Gecko", which meant he would appear on screen as the older brother of "Richard Gecko", played by Tarantino. The role reportedly netted him a modest salary of $250,000.

Right: George played an altogether different character from Dr Ross in the crime/horror movie *From Dusk Till Dawn*.

He and Tarantino were to play brothers on a crime spree, who rob a bank in Texas and head for the Mexican border where they will make a rendezvous with their connection, "Carlos", at the Titty

Twister bar. Along the way, they end up
committing further crimes at a liquor
store and then finally a motel, where
they take "Pastor Jake Fuller" (played
by Harvey Keitel) and his two children
(Juliette Lewis, Ernest Liu) hostage. Once
they reach the Titty Twister bar, up to
their eyeballs in trouble, the last thing
they're expecting is to cross paths with
a town of vicious vampires. It's classic
Tarantino, a vivid homage to countless
b-movies. To make himself get into the
headspace of Seth Gecko, George cut his
hair very short. He must have had no idea
that the so-called 'Roman haircut', would
further enhance his pin-up status, when
he wore it – fresh off work on Rodriguez's
film - in season two of E.R.

The shoot was tight: only eight weeks
long. Filming, which took place in
locations in Mexico, California, Texas and
Washington state, started in June 1995
and wrapped on schedule two months
later, on 20 August 1995. At first, George

was working full time on the film. Then,
once season two of E.R. began shooting,
he was racing back and forth between the
two projects, alternately Dr Ross and Seth
Gecko. When the film came out, George
revealed he often got confused and when
characters would be killed while shooting
From Dusk Till Dawn, he'd automatically
switch into Dr Ross mode and want
to leap into action and save their lives
. . . and that on the set of E.R., he'd be
shooting a scene in which he'd be treating
a child and hand him or her a lollipop
and then the character of Seth Gecko
would take over the moment and he'd
have to bite his lip to stop from uttering,
"take it you little fuck!"

The film was a giant learning curve
for George. Within a year, he had gone
from crisis point, freshly divorced, living
at Richard Kind's house, working on
Sisters and appearing as a "lip syncing
tranvestite" in The Harvest, to being a
star in one of TV's biggest new shows

and now, on top of that, he was fulfilling his years-long dream of breaking into Hollywood. And not only was he shooting a film, but it was a film attached to the golden name of Quentin Tarantino. More than that, it meant acting opposite legendary Method actor, Harvey Keitel, veteran star of films like *Mean Streets*, *Taxi Driver*, *Fingers*, *Bad Lieutenant*, *The Piano* and, of course, *Reservoir Dogs*. George told *Flicks* in 1996, what it was like working opposite such a legend: "I was scared to death. My character was supposed to dominate him. Now, nobody but nobody dominates Harvey on screen. I did my best, but when I look at the result, I can see him throw in a gesture, raise an eyebrow or even take a pause and he takes focus. That's why he's Harvey Keitel and I'm just a lucky guy with the best job in the world."

Once the film wrapped, George went back to being only ridiculously busy instead of insanely, unsustainably busy. He later said that for forty days straight, he worked seven days a week. It was not unusual during this time for George to come off working on *From Dusk Till Dawn* in the early hours of the morning and go to work on *E.R.* at dawn.

Back at work on *E.R.* in the autumn, the buzz about *From Dusk Till Dawn*, was great news for George's collateral in the movie business. His agent began to receive serious interest. Then a major proposal came through. Dreamworks SKG, the production company, founded by Steven Spielberg, David Geffen and Jeffrey Katzenberg in late 1994, was now ready to greenlight its first feature film production – a thriller provisionally titled *The Peacemaker*, based on a work of journalism by Andrew Cockburn and Leslie Cockburn, which investigated the smuggling of nuclear weapons in Russia.

Spielberg, having served as an Executive Producer during the launch era of *E.R.*, knew George's talent and felt he was perfectly suited for the part of "Lt. Colonel Thomas Devoe".

This would give George the male lead. The part came to him via personal communication from none other than Spielberg himself, as he later told *Movieline*: "Steven Spielberg sent me a note, saying, *The Peacemaker* is the first film from our new studio and I'd love you to do it." That blew George's mind. Then he learned of what Spielberg was offering in terms of money: $3 million. A radical hike from the $250,000 he'd been offered for *From Dusk Till Dawn*.

Then, in a double stroke of luck, George was offered another role – that of "Jack Taylor" in *One Fine Day*, a romantic comedy directed by Michael Hoffman. This was a huge break and the part would see George acting

Above: Georege's first multi-million dollar pay cheque came in *The Peacemaker*.

Above: George with
Michelle Pfeiffer in the
romantic comedy *One
Fine Day.*

opposite Michelle Pfeiffer, playing
"Melanie Parker". The story concerned
Parker, a divorced architect and mother
and her crossing of paths with Taylor, a
divorced newspaper columnist and father.
She knows of him because he is her best
friend's ex-husband. They both miss a
ferry which will be taking their children
on their way to a school field trip. She
needs somebody to look after her son
while she attends a very important work
meeting. He's looking after his daughter
because his ex has headed off on her

honeymoon and is up to his eyeballs in
trouble because of a column he wrote.
After bickering, they conclude to share
the day's childcare duty. He covers for her
and then she for him.

Although at first they seem mutually
embittered towards the institution of
marriage and unlikely to be in the mood
for love for years to come, little by little,
they soften towards each other until the
inevitable happens. As a movie, it has
all the hallmarks of an old fashioned
romance. But a contemporary one, in

words. Michelle's comments to him were reportedly, "Kind of cute, one of Dedee's boyfriends, yeah, OK, nice to meet you."

When his name came up for the part, on the back of the massive success of *E.R.*, Pfeiffer knew what to expect – "He's a little bit of a smart-alec but in a charming kind of way and he could do this part. Yeah. Good idea."

It was not hard for George to access the character's romantic status. Having been divorced himself, he knew the panorama of feelings all too well. Not that he was still single and mourning. He was well and truly over the misery of his divorce from Talia Balsam and was now linked with actress Kimberly Russell. She was born in December 1964 and, at the time she met George, had a string of TV roles to her credit. Her older sister, Lisa Marie Russell, is also an actress. The relationship with George, however, was short lived.

Meanwhile, the second season of *E.R.* raged on. George had been nominated for an Emmy in the category of "Outstanding Lead Actor in a Drama Series". He lost out to Dennis Franz for his work in *NYPD Blue*.

which parents of both genders have hectic careers in a working environment that does not allow for the kind of flexibility modern working parents so desperately need.

George was signed up for the film partly because Michelle Pfeiffer, also wearing the hat of executive producer for the project, thought he was well suited. She had met him in the 1980s, when he briefly dated her sister, Dedee Pfeiffer. Back then, according to CNN, they had barely exchanged more than a few

Above: Following his divorce from Talia Balsam, George was soon being romantically linked with actress Kimberly Russell.

dumped at his feet made for compulsive viewing. The more he challenged the system, the more the viewers cheered him on, while waiting nervously, hands over eyes, for the inevitable fallout. It came in an episode on 2 November, in which Dr Greene and Dr Carter learn that Dr Ross has slept with a medical student, Harper Tracy. When the indiscretion reaches top management, Bernstein, Dr Ross is threatened with being fired from the hospital.

Two episodes later, airing on 19 November, Dr Ross decides to leave County General. He has been offered a job in the far better-paying private paediatric sector and is close to committing to the shift. Then, after what he believes to have been his last *E.R.* shift, he is driving through torrential rain, when he gets a puncture. A young boy happens upon Dr Ross and asks for help – his brother's life is in danger. Dr Ross follows the boy and improvises various medical procedures to keep the boy's brother alive until he can be rushed to the *E.R.* There, Dr Ross' everyday colleagues are impressed by what he did out in the field, without medical supplies or surgical tools. The episode, titled "Hell And High Water", was a showcase for George – and for his character. In the following episode, which went out on 16 November 1995, Dr Ross is permitted back into County's fold by Bernstein, on account of his rescue. Later in the same episode, Dr Ross, not long the hero with a halo, receives a phone call from his estranged father and turns up to an awards ceremony drunk. It's typical Dr Ross – tumbling from one crisis to the next.

Late in 1995, George was rumoured to have a new woman on his arm. He had broken up with Kimberly Russell and the gossip was that he was seeing another actress – Karen Duffy. She was born on 23 May 1961 in New York City. When she and George met, she had appeared in films such as Spike Lee's *Malcolm X*, Ben Stiller's Generation X film, *Reality*

Emmy or no Emmy, the great work continued. In an episode airing on 5 October 1995, Dr Ross won yet more female fans when he treated a four-year-old Asian boy who comes into the *E.R.* with symptoms soon diagnosed as AIDS. It was a textbook episode of *E.R.* in terms of understanding what it was about Dr Ross that appealed to so many. Heroic and rebellious, male viewers wanted to be him; female viewers just wanted him.

Viewers grew used to knowing they could count on Dr Ross to go out on a limb for the underdog, to buck the system if it helped make someone's life even a dot better. Led by his heart, his pursuit of an honest response to every calamity

Bites and Farrelly Brothers' *Dumb And Dumber*. Before that, she had modelled and found success as a popular VJ for MTV, known as "Duff". She and George were linked across late 1995 and early 1996. During that year, 1996, she began having headaches. Ten months after the first headache, she was diagnosed with sarcoidosis, a rare and incurable disease that attacks the central nervous system. In Karen's case, it was affecting her brain. Following some time out for extensive treatment, Karen was to return to her acting career, write books about her experiences, get married and start a family. In an interview with *Esquire* magazine in 2007, George finally quashed all rumours about a relationship with Karen, stating simply that, "... she's one of my dearest friends."

Back in the E.R., George had a less dominant role in the show for the latter part of season two. His character continued to stick up for the underdog. And kept clashing with authority – bust ups with Dr Greene and Dr Benton both featured before the season ended. The script writers brought in his father and mother, who appeared in different episodes, lending extra depth to his troubled character.

Mid season, on 19 January 1996, *From Dusk Till Dawn* opened at cinemas across the U.S. The film was a modest success – taking just over $10 million over its opening weekend. It went on to gross just under $26 million in the U.S. and a further $33 million in the rest of the world. The film ended up earning George the "Best Breakthrough Performance" award in the 1996 MTV Movie Awards. Reviews were strong. *Variety* dubbed it a "deliriously trashy, exuberantly vulgar, lavishly appointed exploitation picture" and singled out George's sudden star power as a key factor in the film, "From the first scene, it is clear that the *E.R.* sensation, who has made numerous forgettable pics in the past, has the looks, authority and action-film savvy to

be a new Clark Gable or Mad Max fold Mel Gibson." *Time* magazine also came out with a positive verdict for George, declaring, "He seizes the screen and melts it." George was ecstatic. Already a TV star and now a movie star in the making, the critical acclaim he craved was finally within his grasp.

Above: In late 1995 George was falsely rumoured to have a new love in his life, actress Karen Duffy.

5

WORKING FROM DUSK TILL DAWN

Back to back with working on the last cluster of episodes in season two of *E.R.*, George arrived in New York on 26 February 1996, to start shooting *One Fine Day*. He had struck a deal with *E.R.* executive producer, John Wells, whereby all scenes featuring Dr Ross could be shot in a sequence that allowed him to flit back and forth between East and West Coasts without disrupting the production schedules either of *E.R.* or *One Fine Day*. The accommodating nature of *E.R.*'s producers is a clear indicator of how brightly George's star was beginning to shine.

The shoot went well, working its way slowly up to the peak of the film, a scene in which George and Michelle Pfeiffer's characters finally kiss. Of filming that scene, George told CNN, "You always see these people, yeah, it's so embarrassing, all these people standing around watching you, it's so difficult. No. You get to kiss Michelle Pfeiffer. How difficult is that? I used to cut tobacco for a living, now I'm kissing Michelle Pfeiffer."

It was a typical George quip. As his media coverage grew, he was becoming increasingly self-deprecatory. The years of striving meant his star stayed in check. He wasn't about to suddenly mutate into an egotistical movie star. He made it clear in his interviews that he had his feet firmly on the ground and that he took neither himself nor his sudden fame too seriously.

Despite that easy-come, easy-go public image, he was not at all happy with the paparazzi and press attention that accompanied his new-found celebrity. He told CNN in December 1996 that during the filming of *One Fine Day*, his every move was being pursued to such

an extent that he had to sneak out of his trailer to get onto the set of the film. During that year, he lashed out often and publicly at celebrity gossip vehicles, like the tabloid TV news show, *Hard Copy* and tried to rally fellow Hollywood stars to join him in boycotting *Hard Copy* and fellow Paramount show, *Entertainment Tonight*.

Of course, weeks before, his star had leaped to a new unimagined height. Warner Bros had run into trouble in February, with the casting of a sequel to *Batman Forever*, which would eventually become *Batman & Robin*, directed by Joel Schumacher. It was believed that Val Kilmer and Chris O'Donnell were set to reprise their roles. However, Kilmer decided that he didn't want to appear in the sequel. Apparently, within a week of Kilmer's final decision, Warner Bros had approached George, met with him and offered him the role of "Batman".

The *One Fine Day* shoot ended on 18 May 1996. Two days earlier, the finale to season two of *E.R.* had gone out on NBC. Amazingly, ten days after finishing *One Fine Day*, George arrived on the set of *The Peacemaker*. The film was directed by Mimi Leder, a New Yorker,

Previous spread:
George with his hands full during the filming of *One Fine Day*.
Right: Ten days after completing filming on *One Fine Day*, George was on set for *The Peacemaker*.

Above: George finds
an unorthodox way to
take a taxi in New York
during filming of *The
Peacemaker*.

who had helmed various episodes of *E.R.* as well serving as supervising producer during the first season. She had directed multiple made-for-TV films as well as episodes of TV shows like *L.A. Law.* The plot was straightforward: army Special Forces expert, Lt Colonel Thomas Devoe (George) and White House nuclear scientist, Dr Julia Kelly (Nicole Kidman), are assigned to investigate an alleged accident in which a military train carrying an armed nuclear warhead crashes into a passenger train and explodes in Russia. The White House believes it was the work of terrorists.

The film, whose budget has been estimated as being close to $50 million, had a diverse list of locations – Slovakia, Czech Republic, Poland, Croatia, Austria and several U.S. cities. While in Europe, in August, George was enjoying some leisure time in Paris. At a party in a country house, he met a waitress. She was Celine Balitran, a law student. She said she worked at a bar. The bar turned out to be at the hip nightclub, Barfly. Smitten, George went to Barfly and asked her out. They went out on a date, hitting it off in a major way. When George went back to Los Angeles, the interest continued. They called each other and he invited her out to California. When she arrived at Casa de Clooney, the attraction was even stronger. Officially dating, George suggested she move in with him. And so it was, two and a half weeks after they first locked eyes at Barfly, Celine made the decision to return to Paris, pack her bags and move permanently to Los Angeles.

George had just bought Casa de Clooney, an eight-bedroom house, and already it was a hangout for the actor and the boys. The mock Tudor house sat on three and a half acres of land and was surrounded by an electronic fence. It had

a swimming pool, a basketball court and a tennis court. Located in the foothills of Studio City, in the Hollywood Hills, it had an interesting history. It had once been owned by Fleetwood Mac legend and solo artist, Stevie Nicks and more recently rented by white rapper Vanilla Ice.

The Peacemaker shoot would go on until 18 September 1996. When he came off that shoot, George was already hard at work filming his third feature film of 1996 – *Batman & Robin*, which started shooting on 12 September. The pace was relentless. He was working obsessively, clawing his way back to a sense of equilibrium in his mind, trying to get to a place where he felt his success was sufficient for his age. He was now 35 years old and making up for lost time, those long twelve years of building a career as an actor for himself, audition by audition, part by part, rejection by rejection, triumph by triumph.

Constantly on camera, he was careful to look after himself. He got into a habit of eating only an apple for breakfast, to help keep his weight down and he worked out when he had time, using a rowing machine. The austere breakfast and exercise regime cancelled out the calorie blast of his favourite dinner at the time – pasta with marinara sauce.

Jumping from film project to project was only part of the fever. A third season of *E.R.* was now active. The first episode aired on 26 September 1996. This meant George was racing back and forth between the sets of *E.R.* and *Batman & Robin*.

In season three, Dr Ross continued to wear his heart on his sleeve. In an episode going out on 17 October, he rushes into the E.R., with a one night stand in his arms. She's had an epileptic seizure. When his colleagues ask him for her name, regarding admissions forms, he can't even remember. It's another moment where the reactions of others make it seem as though his life is out of control.

Throughout this season, as before, the "will they, won't they" storyline concerning Dr Ross and Carol Hathaway kept ticking over. In an episode that went out on Halloween, Dr Ross and Carol go out together, staffing a mobile healthcare vehicle, helping the underprivileged and homeless. Once again, Dr Ross' big heart is at the centre of the episode. Struggling always to care for one person, he never fails to care for humanity at large.

On 20 December 1996, *One Fine Day* opened at cinemas in the U.S. *The Washington Post* called it an "appealing, if overcooked romantic comedy". *Entertainment Weekly* zoomed in on George, using the film to analyse whether he could make the leap from TV star to movie star and came through with a dazzling verdict: "Clooney proves himself to be a true movie star and romantic leading man. His charm, his energy, even his ease with children (one of any adult actor's most terrifying challenges) carry *One Fine Day* into irresistibility." The review in *EW* also succinctly nailed the secret ingredient of his pin-up appeal, "Clooney's brand of sexiness – a bemused awareness that he turns the girls on, tempered by the self-knowledge that the results are often far more trouble than they're worth – is a variation on his *E.R.* character." Some reviews were less positive, citing how long it takes for the characters to get together as a flaw in

Above: George's co-star in *The Peacemaker* was Nicole Kidman.
Left: *The Peacemaker* gave George the chance to play a uniformed, all-action hero, but here was a different uniform and even more action waiting in the wings.

the film. Others complained of the film's earnest bid for social topicality. Overall, the film was a box office hit, grossing $46 million in the U.S. and a further $51 million worldwide. George later summed the film up, to *Movieline*, as follows: "It wasn't groundbreaking stuff, but it makes you smile. And it made a lot of money. Was it a great film? Absolutely not. Was I proud to be in it and was it a lucky break for me? Absolutely."

1997 arrived with George still working seven days a week, eighteen hours a day. The third season of *E.R.* continued to win ever swelling viewing figures. In 1996, he had again been nominated for an Emmy for his work as Dr Ross, same as the year before, in the category of "Outstanding Lead Actor in a Drama Series". Finally, the overload came to an end. On 27 January, the *Batman & Robin* shoot wrapped and George was able to go back to merely working on *E.R.* – in itself a demanding proposition.

The only consolation for George was that he had sworn off any other film projects for the time being. He would just concentrate on *E.R.* And that was the way it stayed from late January until spring, when he shot the last episode of the third season. The finale aired on 15 May 1997 and teased viewers in the extreme because it featured that long-

hoped-for kiss between Dr Ross and Carol Hathaway. It then left millions on the edge of their sofas, wondering whether the serial womaniser and commitment-phobe would actually settle down with Carol.

A month later, on 12 June, *Batman & Robin* opened at cinemas across the U.S. George held his breath, waiting for the critical verdict. Reviews were damning, though more of the film than of George specifically. *Variety* said, "Physically, Clooney is unquestionably the most ideal Batman to date, but none of the series' screenwriters has ever gotten a handle on how to make the character as interesting as those around him and Clooney is unable to compensate onscreen for the lack of dimension on paper." They damned the film summarising, "the operative word is bland."

The Washington Post was no less forgiving: "Like a wounded yeti, *Batman & Robin* drags itself through icicle-heavy sets, dry-ice fog and choking jungle vines, before dying in a frozen heap. Unfortunately, that demise occurs about 20 minutes into the movie, which leaves you in the cold for approximately 106 minutes." Janet Maslin, reviewing the film for *The New York Times*, wrote that George's Batman was "played affably but blandly."

Roger Ebert, writing for *The Chicago Sun Times*, said of George's turn as the caped crusader, "I've always suspected they cast movie Batmans by their chins, which is all you see when the Bat costume is being worn and Clooney has the best chin yet. But like Michael Keaton and Val Kilmer, he brings nothing much to the role because there's nothing much there. Most of the time he seems stuck for conversation." And finally, a particularly harsh review of George's performance appeared in *The San Francisco Chronicle*, "George Clooney is the big zero of the film and should go down in history as the George Lazenby of the series. Beyond the sheer bad luck of looking 20 years older in his Batmask, Clooney – he's not a doctor but he plays one on TV – makes

Right: George and Chris O'Donnell in *Batman and Robin*. Below: Alicia Silverston joined the caped crusaders as "Batgirl" for the new movie.

a smug, complacent, one-dimensional Caped Crusader." It doesn't stop there. The review then moves to specific complaints, "Clooney tries to make Batman a smooth dude. Also warm and fuzzy. He looks at people as if he's deeply sensitive and might say something nice if only he weren't so cool. Then he does his head-shake thing. Whenever Clooney wants to seem sincere here, he nods his head this way and that. It's as emotionally convincing as Bill Clinton biting his bottom lip."

Despite the torrent of negative reviews, audiences flocked to see the latest film in the series. Against an estimated budget of $122 million, the film took $107 million at the U.S. box office and a further $130 million worldwide. A substantial gross, but a failure compared to 1995's *Batman Forever*, with Val Kilmer as Batman, which grossed $336 million worldwide.

George found the bad reviews crushing. He'd never really had anything but positive press up to this point. He later said, "I'd never been thumped before. So I took it hard."

In the aftermath, he conceded that it was a "pretty horrendous film" and that the elements just weren't stellar, "None of us really did it right. I got a call from Joel (Schumacher) right after I made the deal for *The Peacemaker* and he said, 'Do you want to play Batman in the next film?' And I jumped up and down, screamed and said, 'Yes, I will play Batman!' I thought it was a bad script. But again, a gigantic break. Batman changed everything. Without Batman,

I wouldn't ever have gotten to do *Out of Sight*. And as bad as it was, *Batman & Robin* was still a gigantic hit."

George threw himself into working on *E.R.* during those early months of 1997, letting the craziness of the past year cool down, letting his creative energies recharge. After the critical mauling he and *Batman & Robin* picked up, he decided that from that point on, he'd only commit to projects of which he could be 100 per cent proud.

Soon enough, such a project came along in the guise of *Out Of Sight*. Adapted from a story by Elmore Leonard, the film was slated to be directed by Steven Soderbergh, then best known for his U.S. independent directorial debut, *Sex, Lies and Videotape*, which had starred James Spader and Andie MacDowell. Just under two years younger than George, the director was born in Atlanta, Georgia, in 1963 and shared George's taste for cinema of the 1960s and early 1970s. The actor and director found they had much in common and quickly became close friends.

George was to play the role of "Jack Foley", a convicted bank robber who escapes from jail, kidnapping a U.S. marshal, "Karen Sisco", played by singer, model and actress Jennifer Lopez. Along the way, the pair fall in love. Filming started on 1 October 1997, on locations across the U.S. The budget was an estimated $48 million.

A week earlier, on 26 September 1997, *The Peacemaker* had opened at U.S. cinemas. The film grossed $41 million in the U.S. against an estimated $50 million budget and went on to take a further $69 million worldwide. Reviews were mixed. Not damning, the way reviews for *Batman & Robin* were damning, but lukewarm nonetheless. In the back of George's mind, was the fear that his Hollywood spree would dry out and he'd be jettisoned back to TV. The double critical assault on *Batman & Robin* and then *The Peacemaker* surprised him.

Salon.com, for instance, said of his turn in *The Peacemaker*, "the character of the take-charge army guy does nothing for Clooney. He basically is called on to act cocky throughout the entire movie." Roger Ebert, again reviewing for *The Chicago Sun Times*, said: "This is the first big release from the new DreamWorks studio and it looks great. The technical credits are impeccable, and Clooney and Kidman negotiate assorted dangers skilfully. But it's mostly spare parts from other thrillers." And this was what George came to feel; that the film was reviewed as the launch title from Dreamworks, more than it was reviewed as a feature film; that the business ambitions of Spielberg, Geffen and Katzenberg were being critiqued and analysed; that all of his own efforts were being overshadowed and dismissed.

Two sets of bad reviews underlined George's philosophy of success. He had travelled a long way to reach the place he was now in professionally. He was disappointed and shaken, as anyone would be. But he was also, sagely, saying, "I didn't really get famous until I was 33 years old. I had almost been famous several times. There's a great lesson in that, which is that it has very little to do with you. I don't know if you can figure that out as easily when you're 23, because you think you're the smartest person in the room."

To offset the bashing, George received good news in November 1997. *People* magazine slapped George on their cover and pronounced him the "Sexiest Man Alive". The annual award, which had launched in 1985, underscored his broad appeal.

Having found one man with his heart in the cinema in Steven Soderbergh, George crossed paths with another in Terrence Malick, the director of *Days Of Heaven* and *Badlands*, two classics of seventies American cinema. When George heard that the notoriously reclusive director was planning on making a third film, *The Thin Red Line*,

Right: George was back in military fatigues in 1997 for his role in Terrence Malick's *Thin Red Line*.

he joined a lengthy queue of admiring actors, led by Sean Penn and Woody Harrelson, who wanted a part in the military drama.

He arranged to meet with Malick, who would be shooting the film between June and December 1997, mostly on location in Australia. "When I heard Terrence was making a new movie, I let it be known that, hell, I'd carry film boxes. I just wanted to be able to say that somewhere down the line I worked with Terrence Malick." After the meeting, Malick offered George various scenes, which amounted to two days work. He flew down to Australia, shot the scenes, left. He has spoken since of the experience being "intimidating", on account of finding himself working with Malick and the likes of Sean Penn, whom George greatly admires. The finished film only briefly featured George. But it was enough to satisfy the actor. The project, along with working with Soderbergh, gave him the sense of kudos for which he was so hungry. The projects endorsed his passion for acting, his bid to be seen as one of the great American actors of his generation.

George, had not, however, lost his sense of fun. Next, he lent his voice to the character "Sparky The Dog" in an episode of *South Park* which aired on 3 September 1997, titled "Big Gay Al's Big Gay Boat Ride". The episode was the fourth in the first season.

As of 25 September, *E.R.* was back on

NBC. The fourth season launched that evening and once more, George was juggling work on *E.R.* with work on a feature film: *Out of Sight*.

George had worked three seasons of his five-season *E.R.* contract. When his contract came up for renegotiation, he refused to ask for more money. It was an old-fashioned principle. The show had made him a star, opened the door to Hollywood. He would always be appreciative of the break. After the contract renegotiations were complete, he was being paid the lowest salary out of any of the regulars on the show, despite having risen to become (arguably) the show's biggest star. He said his father applauded this honorable way of doing business.

The new season opened with the introduction of a British doctor character – "Elizabeth Corday". The new episodes made good, too, on that kiss between Dr Ross and Carol at the end of season three. In the second episode of the new season, Dr Ross makes a gesture towards his serious feelings for Carol, by suggesting he has a drawer at her home for his overnight items. Viewers loved his tentative step towards commitment.

Over the coming episodes, Dr Ross's father dies and he heads out to California to deal with the paperwork, with Dr Greene riding along for moral support. Meanwhile, the Dr Ross-Carol plotline flourishes, leading to the couple going public on their relationship. As the season rolled into 1998, Dr Ross and Carol were on to discussing deepening their commitment. The season finale came on 14 May 1998, with Dr Ross hauled before Dr Greene and Weaver for trying, with Carol's help, to detox an infant addicted to methadone through his mother's drugs habit, without the mother's permission. It was the zenith of Dr Ross's problems.

Midway through that season, *Out of Sight* finished shooting on 12 January 1998, halving George's workload until spring. For the next four months,

he was once again focused on *E.R.*, the long hours, the hectic shoots, the choreography of each scene and the complex medical-speak required for the role. There were rumours, as there had been since 1996, that George was thinking of leaving the show. This time George confirmed that it was true. He would shoot one last season, the fifth, before leaving TV solely to pursue a career in feature films.

An oddity on the second half of his resumé, George made a guest appearance in the TV show *Murphy Brown*. His part, that of "Doctor 2" aired in an episode that went out on 18 May 1998. This was not just any ordinary episode of the hit TV show, though. It was the last-ever episode, the finale of a ten-season run in which Candice Bergen had consistently played a journalist who co-anchors a network news show.

On 26 June 1998, *Out of Sight* was released to U.S. cinemas. It was not the ideal time for a film like this to come out, but into the light summer release schedule it went. Despite the unfortunate release date, reviews were good. One of the best came from Mick La Salle, reviewing for *The San Francisco Chronicle*. The same critic who had savaged George in *Batman & Robin*, was now ready to praise him. Under the headline, "Clooney Breaks Out", he wrote, "*Out of Sight* may go down in the annals of film as the movie in which George Clooney learned how to keep his head still – and became a leading man. What a difference. Until now he's been unable to say a line of dialogue without his head bobbing and weaving as though it were at the end of a fishing line. Suddenly, he's

able to stand still, look the other actor in the eye and speak. He has authority and presence and because he's not trying to look cute, he has never looked better." He went on to pronounce the film a "minor masterpiece".

Despite strong reviews, the film battled the holiday season and didn't attract as big an audience as it should have done, considering both Jennifer Lopez and George were such hot property at this time. The film ended up grossing around $37 million in the U.S. and $78 million worldwide. It was a reasonable take for a film with an estimated budget of $48 million – but by Hollywood standards, hardly a massive success.

George had a brief holiday that summer from his recent workload and spent it with Celine Balitran. The couple had by now been together two years – George's most serious relationship since his marriage to Talia Balsam. Sustaining such a relationship was complex, as George's work schedule remained incessantly hectic. If he wasn't shooting *E.R.* or a film, then he was preparing for *E.R.* or a film, or promoting *E.R.* or a film.

And then it was back to work on his fifth and final season of *E.R.* late that summer. The season premiere went out on 24 September 1998. The emphasis was still on Dr Ross and Carol's relationship. A few episodes into the new season, Carol thinks she might be pregnant. This prepares the way for a climax of sorts in the dalliance between the two characters. The storyline needed to exit carefully, so as not to jeopardise the future of the show. Slowly, the writers eased Dr Ross from the show. The first indication of this came in the first episode of 1999, when Dr Ross receives a job offer, which would involve him leaving Chicago and relocating to Portland, Oregon.

In general, though, Dr Ross was up to his usual tricks, giving sample drugs to desperately sick patients, forging paperwork to help a patient get better

Right: George was to leave behind his *E.R.* co-stars at the end of the show's fifth season, although it would not be the last the "County General Hospital" would see of him.

treatment and tampering with a research study. Facing charges, Dr Weaver prohibits him from treating any further patients. Dr Ross resigns and begs Carol to quit too and move with him to the Northwest. She says she can't. He goes anyway. The producers were keen for George not to exit the show by way of death or a tragic turn of events. Instead, they wanted the door left open, as did George.

He shot that final episode on Thursday 14 January 1999. Afterwards, there was a send-off party in the studio lot. George was presented with a cake bearing his face. Every Friday, the cast and crew had kept up a ritual called Dollar Day, when they all dropped $1 in a box. And at the end of the day, in a raffle of names, someone on set took home $100 or so. This last time, George called it on Thursday and dropped a cheque for $5000 in the box. A crew member made the lucky draw. And then the party was over and George walked away from his $42,000 paycheque per episode. By contrast, at this time, Anthony Edwards was apparently earning $375,000 per episode. Cast and crew all told the press they'd miss Dr Ross as well as George's incessant on-set practical jokes and the sight of him endlessly shooting basketball hoops (he'd fitted a hoop on the side of his trailer).

The show would struggle temporarily to adjust to losing George. And then, adding to that first blow, Julianna Margulies announced she would be leaving in the sixth season. Without Dr Ross, she felt Carol would drift. During the rest of that fifth season, once Dr Ross leaves, a subdued Carol reveals that she's pregnant and that Dr Ross does not know. In an episode aired in May 1999, Carol finally tells him that she's carrying twins. The season ended on 20 May. Nobody could have guessed that when Carol exited the show in the following season, George would return to make a hush-hush special guest appearance.

Left: When George hung up Doug Ross's stethoscope, Julianna Margulies also decided that Carol Hathaway was heading for her final shift in E.R.

6

LADIES AND GENTLEMEN, GEORGE CLOONEY, FILM ACTOR

In those last days of *E.R.*, George was already signed up for a new film project, which would overlap with the end of his commitments on the show. The film was *Three Kings*, directed by David O. Russell, whose prior films included *Spanking The Monkey* and *Flirting With Disaster.* For the new film, Russell wrote the screenplay himself, based on a story by John Ridley and envisaged the end result to land somewhere between *M.A.S.H.* and *Kelly's Heroes.*

The film revolves around a small group of soldiers at the end of the Gulf War. Upon finding a map that may lead them to hidden gold, stolen from Kuwait by Saddam Hussein's government, they set off in search of the treasure. Along the way, they encounter Iraqi civilians hoping for U.S. assistance. They face a testing dilemma: do they rescue these fellow human beings, or go in pursuit of the gold which will make them rich?

George was signed up to play "Major Archie Gates", opposite Spike Jonze, Ice Cube and Mark Wahlberg. Russell told SPLICEDwire.com how he came to have George in the film, "George Clooney had a passion for the part. He pursued it. He got a hold of the script before anybody gave it to him and he made a case for it. He was coming off of *Out Of Sight* and was trying to put some of the weaker pictures he'd done behind him and

wanted to work with stronger filmmakers. I was happy to work with him because he'd done strong work in *Out of Sight* and I felt he was ready to do it again." Before signing George, the director had gone after a long list of leading men, including Nicolas Cage and Mel Gibson.

Shooting on the $46 million film began on 12 November 1998. From the word go, George did not like the way Russell worked. He later told *Playboy*, "He yelled and screamed at people all day, from day one."

In the same interview George outlined specific incidents on sets, such as: "Once, he (Russell) went after a camera-car driver who I knew from high school. I had nothing to do with his getting his job, but David began yelling and screaming at him and embarrassing him in front of everybody. I told him, 'You can yell and scream and even fire him, but what you can't do is humiliate him in front of people. Not on my set, if I have any say about it.'"

Previous spread: George as "Major Archie Gates" in *Three Kings*.
Below: George with Mark Wahlberg and Ice Cube on the unhappy set of *Three Kings*.

Above: George with John Turturro and Tim Blake Nelson in the Cohen Brothers' *O Brother Where Art Thou?*

To diffuse the tension, George clowned about on set, as he always did. Russell has said that George's favourite prank at the time was to go around with a water bottle squirting people's butts, so it appeared as though the victim had wet his or her pants.

Despite this par for the course injection of Clooney humour, the static continued. One day, according to George, Russell started screaming at the script supervisor and made her cry. George, a la Dr Ross, felt bad for the woman and wrote Russell a letter, complaining. He told *Playboy*, that it went something like this: "Look, I don't know why you do this. You've written a brilliant script and I think you're a good director. Let's not have a set like this. I don't like it and I don't work well like this."

Then, just when things seemed as though they couldn't get any worse, Russell and George actually came to blows. Three weeks behind schedule, there was a run-in between an army extra and Russell. The extra was meant to knock Ice Cube over but in Russell's opinion he hadn't made a good job of it. George has said that the extra was nervous and that Russell then went over to the extra and pushed him and started shouting at him, "Do you want to be in this f**king movie? Then throw him to the f**king ground!" When the second assistant director objected to the way Russell was behaving he, too, was treated to a stream of abuse at which point George claims he simply replied in kind with "F**k you! I quit!"

George then went over to the director, put his arm around him and tried to talk the situation back down to a calmer level. As George tells it, Russell did not respond well: "He turned on me and said, 'Why don't you just worry about your f**ked-up act? You're being a d**k. You want to hit me? You want to hit me? Come on, pussy, hit me.' I'm looking at him like he's out of

his mind. Then he started banging me on the head with his head. He goes, 'Hit me, you pussy. Hit me.' Then he got me by the throat and I went nuts. I had him by the throat. I was going to kill him. Kill him. Finally, he apologized, but I walked away." The film wrapped on 15 March 1999. George would later refer to the shoot as the "worst experience of my life".

Healing the wound, George then went to a film project on which he loved working – a new Coen Brothers film, called *O Brother Where Art Thou?* The film fitted into the classic jailbreak genre. Vaguely taking cues from Homer's *The Odyssey*, the film was set in 1937 Mississippi and followed three convicts who escape from a chain gang to go on the run, hoping to pick up the hidden loot from the bank heist that got them

banged up. George was cast as "Everett", John Turturro as "Pete" and Tim Blake Nelson as "Delmar". The shoot started on 7 June 1999, on location in Mississippi, with a strong supporting cast including John Goodman and Holly Hunter. The shoot wrapped 23 August.

In tandem, George also started work on another film – *The Perfect Storm*, directed by Wolfgang Petersen, the German director who had recently helmed *In The Line Of Fire*. Playing "Capt Billy Tyne", George was cast opposite Mark Wahlberg. The supporting cast was excellent – John C. Reilly, Karen Allen and Diane Lane.

Based on the bestselling book by Sebastian Junger, the film told the story of a ship, *Andrea Gail*, which sailed from Massachusetts for the North Atlantic fishing grounds in 1991 and ran into a

Left: George split up with Celine Balitran after three years, their relationship foundering when Celine decided she wanted to start a family.

Above: *O Brother Where Art Thou?* was a prison break comedy that drew favourable reviews and even comparisons between George and the legendary Clark Gable.

Right: George filmed the gentle comedy *O Brother Where Art Thou?* and the tense drama *The Perfect Storm* simultaneously.

horrific storm. George's character, along with Wahlberg's, is desperate for a more prolific fishing season, so he advocates sailing into seasonally risque waters in the hope of netting a major haul. They make a big catch, but then, faced with the ice machine breaking down, they have to get it back to port as quickly as possible. This means sailing through a forecasted storm. They have no idea how enormous the storm is and sail into it, with disastrous consequences.

The film started shooting on 26 July 1999, which meant that, once again, George was shooting two projects simultaneously.

Also featuring in that hectic summer, *South Park Bigger Longer & Uncut* opened at U.S, cinemas on 30 June, featuring George's voice for the character of "Dr Gouache". It was his second affiliation with the show.

Meanwhile, all was not well on the domestic front. George and Celine Balitran's three-year relationship had come to an end and she had moved out of Casa de Clooney. She later told French weekly, *Oh! La*, why they split up: "I wanted to have a real family with children. But it will never be the right time for George."

George felt bad about the relationship coming to an end and did his best to set her up with a comfortable future. "She pulled up roots and came here for me. So I felt it became something of my responsibility to make sure that, even though we're not still together, her life is not bad because of that. So I made sure that she had a great place to live. And I made sure that she had cash. And I still talk to her and make sure that she has a lawyer who will help her with her visa."

When the dust settled, he later blamed the breakup on his infamous workaholism, telling *The Sunday Mirror*, "It definitely did ruin my relationship with Celine (Balitran) several years back. So I suppose I have decided to prioritise my life in such a way that work takes precedence, if it means

Above: *The Perfect Storm* told the story of a fishing boat crew fighting the elements to land a profitable catch.

I won't be able to see someone I've been involved with for two or three months at a time, that's the kind of decision I've made regarding my life."

Three Kings opened on 3 October 1999 and drew $15 million over its opening weekend before going on to gross somewhere in the region of $60 million in the U.S. and a further $47 million throughout the rest of the world. Reviews were favourable. *The San Francisco Chronicle* called it, "George Clooney's best showcase to date." *Salon* weren't quite as smitten, though, saying, "Clooney's virile, slightly dissolute charm is intact throughout *Three Kings* but I think he's wasted without a woman to slither around."

Meanwhile George, fresh out of his breakup from Celine Balitran, was reportedly seeing the actress Brooke Langton. The 29-year-old, born in Arizona in November 1970, had recently finished a two-year stint as "Samantha Reilly" on hit TV show, *Melrose Place*. She had also appeared in Doug Liman's cult 1996 film, *Swingers* as well as playing a small part on *Chicago Hope* – *E.R.*'s onetime medical drama rival. By all accounts, the relationship was short-lived, over in a matter of months.

On 23 December 1999, George finished work on *The Perfect Storm* and over Christmas, prepared himself for his next

project – a one-off TV show produced
by his own, recently founded production
company, Maysville Productions. That
year, Maysville had already produced
Kilroy, a TV comedy pilot about the life
of an aspiring actor, for Warner Bros TV
and HBO. Like so many pilots George
had worked on in the past as an actor, the
show never materialised.

The new project was *Fail Safe*. It was
pitched as a live televised play based
on the 1962 novel *Fail-Safe*, by Eugene
Burdick and Harvey Wheeler. The novel,
an account of a cold war era crisis, had
already formed the basis for Sidney
Lumet's 1964 film. The remake, directed
by Stephen Frears, would go out live on

CBS in black and white.

Along with *Three Kings*, it marked
the beginnings of George's political
conscience, inherited from his father,
crossing over into his professional life.
The plot revolved around a U.S. bomber
plane given incorrect instructions to
drop a nuclear bomb on Moscow. George
rallied big names like Harvey Keitel,
E.R. pal Noah Wyle, Brian Dennehy
and Richard Dreyfuss casting them
alongside himself (in a brief showing) as
well as appearances by two of 'the Boys':
Grant Heslov and Tommy Hinkley. The
show, which went out on 9 April 2000,
became the first live fictional show
broadcast on CBS in three decades. In

Above: Mark Wahlberg
and George prepare
for a drenching in *The
Perfect Storm.*

Above: Brad Pitt, Matt Damon, Elliot Gould and Don Cheadle line up alongside George in *Ocean's Eleven*.
Right: George synchronizes watches with Matt Damon in *Ocean's Eleven*.

2001, it deservedly won two Emmy's for "Outstanding Lighting Direction" and "Outstanding Technical Direction, Camerawork, Video for a Miniseries, Movie or a Special". The show was also nominated for a Golden Globe in 2001, in the "Best Mini-Series or Motion Picture Made for TV" category.

In May 2000, George made that hush-hush surprise guest appearance in *E.R.* It remained an industry secret right up until 11 May, when the episode went out in the usual *E.R.* time slot. It was the farewell show for Julianna Marguiles. After resuscitating a terminally ill cancer patient so she can say a final goodbye to her loved ones, Carol realises that she must be with Dr Ross, who, throughout the season, has been pressuring her to leave Chicago and join him in Seattle. Finally she heads for Seattle, where she finds Dr Ross.

George shot the scene in utmost secrecy. Not even his agent knew about it until the last minute. The couple who owned the house that they used to shoot the scene were given a pre-dated cheque for $10,000 for renting their property on the understanding that if they mentioned what was happening to anybody, especially the media, then the cheque would be rendered void. And so it happened that George turned up in *E.R.* again.

The same month, *O Brother Where Art Thou?* premiered at the Cannes Film Festival, later opening at cinemas in the U.S. on 22 December. Reviews were glowing. *Rolling Stone* said of the film, "*O Brother, Where Art Thou?* transports Homer's Odyssey to 1937 Mississippi with an ear-candy score of bluegrass, gospel and country and a live-wire star

turn from George Clooney as a vain escaped convict who wears a hairnet."

The New York Times also zoomed in on George's role, saying, "This film has at its center an elusive, highly mannered performance that appears to belong, as much as the vintage roadsters and ice-cream suits, to a vanished era. Mr. Clooney not only looks like Clark Gable, with his hair slicked against his scalp and his carefully etched Art Deco mustache, but he also gives the kind of detached, matinee-idol performance that used to be Gable's trademark."

It seemed that George, out of *E.R.* and TV shows altogether, was starting to be taken very seriously as a film actor – a fact driven home in 2001 by him winning a Golden Globe for his work in the film when he picked up the "Best Performance by an Actor in a Motion Picture Comedy/ Musical" award. The film also fared well commercially. Against a $26 million budget, it grossed $45 million in the U.S., before taking a further $25 million worldwide.

Continuing this major George Clooney season, *The Perfect Storm* opened at U.S. cinemas on 2 July 2000 and took $41 million that weekend alone, despite tepid reviews. It went on to gross a phenomenal $181 million in the U.S. against its estimated $140 million budget. Add to that worldwide earnings – an additional $146 million – and the film was the biggest box office smash with which George Clooney had yet been involved.

The rest of 2000 was devoted to getting a new project off the ground – a remake of *Ocean's Eleven*, the classic 1960 "Rat Pack" film, which starred Frank Sinatra, Dean Martin, Sammy Davis Jr, Peter Lawford and Angie Dickinson. The film was to be produced by Section Eight, a new production company co-founded by George and Steven Soderbergh who was also to direct the new movie. At the time he was hot from the success of *Erin Brockovich* and *Traffic*.

The history of Section Eight harked

back to 1999. Soderbergh and George were out to dinner at Jones in Hollywood, talking as usual about their favourite period of cinema – 1965-1975 – and their favourite directors: Stanley Kubrick, Francis Ford Coppola, Martin Scorsese and Sidney Lumet. During the evening, George mentioned that he was seeking a new producing partner, that things weren't going as well with Maysville as he wanted. Soderbergh suggested himself. They then sketched out a business plan and took it to Warner Bros, who immediately expressed interest in working with them. Consequently, in early 2000, the giant signed a deal with Section Eight and gave them an office on the Warner lot.

Once the idea for *Ocean's Eleven* was active, they hooked up with producer Jerry Weintraub and hired Ted Griffin to write a screenplay for the remake. Griffin had previously written *Ravenous* and *Best Laid Plans*. The biggest headache for the project revolved around its inherent nature as an ensemble piece with an all-star cast. Nobody quite knew how they were going to sign an all-star cast that mirrored the original without saddling the project with four eye-watering salaries of around $20 million a piece. That potentially meant an $80 million budget just for the four lead roles – add to that the rest of the cast, crew, director and so on, not to mention production itself and you had a project with a vast budget. For a remake, that spelled too great a financial risk. The solution came when George announced that he'd do the project for a minimal salary against a take of profits. Weintraub was instantly surprised that an actor of George's stature would be prepared to cut his fee so

Left: George with Lisa Snowdon, the British actress he met while filming a Martini commercial in Europe.

radically. To that lead and with Warner
Bros backing, George and Soderbergh
went about attracting a stellar cast on the
same terms.

First up, they approached Brad Pitt and
he said he would do it. Then Soderbergh,
who had worked with Julia Roberts on
Erin Brockovich, famously sent her the
screenplay, with a $20 bill attached to it
and a note, saying, "I hear you get 20 a
picture these days". She called him up and
said she was in. The casting continued
in this way, with every actor or actress
who came on board, signing up to work
for a radically lower fee than they usually
commanded.

George was, meanwhile, linked with
a new woman – British model, Lisa
Snowdon, whom he met in October 2000
when they shot a European Martini TV
commercial together. Born Lisa Snawdon,
in Welwyn Garden City, in 1971, she
studied at the Italia Conti School of
Performing Arts. When she and George
started dating, she was best known
for appearing in a Kellogg's Special K
commercial and the TV spot for Faberge's
Addiction scent. He was 39, she was 29.

With Matt Damon and Andy
Garcia completing the stellar cast, the
movie started shooting on 11 February
2001. To honour the original, Angie
Dickinson returned to play a cameo
role. And Soderbergh and Weintraub
themselves made fleeting appearances.
Ocean's Eleven quickly became a
Hollywood buzz project. Everybody
wanted to play a part. Much of the
filming took place on location at the
Bellagio Hotel in Las Vegas.

George was playing "Danny Ocean", a
career criminal just out of jail following

Right: George was
the first of an all-star
cast to agree to work
for a minimal fee
on *Ocean's Eleven*,
banking on a share
of the profits instead.

a long sentence. This meant he was
reprising Frank Sinatra's role in the
original. Unreformable, his first desire,
when free, is to plan a massive casino
heist. He wants to rob three of the richest
casinos in Las Vegas, all owned by "Terry
Benedict" (Andy Garcia), who has been
dating Danny's ex-wife, "Tess" (Julia
Roberts) while he's been incarcerated.
The potential booty is $150 million.

To stand a chance of making off with it,
he needs a crack team to support his plan.
Enter "Rusty Ryan" (Brad Pitt), "Basher

Tarr" (Don Cheadle), "Linus Caldwell"
(Matt Damon), "Reuben Tishkoff"
(Elliott Gould), "Saul Bloom" (Carl
Reiner). Eventually, he has an eleven-man
team in place, and kicks the daring heist
into action.

Midway through the *Ocean's Eleven*
shoot, a new Robert Rodriguez film
opened at U.S. cinemas on 18 March. *Spy
Kids*, aimed at a youth audience, starred
Antonio Banderas. The film featured a
tiny cameo from George, who played
"Devlin". Once more, as the film grossed

a copy machine salesman who sings in a tribute band. When the singer of the band to which his band is paying tribute quits, the imitator becomes a real star.

Rock Star opened at cinemas in the U.S. on 7 September 2001 to a very poor reception. The movie suffered from some distinctly unenthusiastic reviews and was no more popular with the general public than it was with the film critics. It grossed a dismal $16 million in the U.S. and only a further $2 million abroad, against an estimated budget of $38 milllion. It was beginning to look like George's famous "Midas Touch" did not extend to everything with which he was involved after all.

Next, George and Soderbergh, as Section Eight, gave the green light to *Welcome to Collinwood*, a film written and directed by Anthony and Joe Russo. A light comedy about a petty criminal who is given the plans for the perfect heist while languishing in prison, the film is a remake of 1958 Italian movie *Big Deal On Madonna Street* and stars William H. Macy, Isaiah Washington and Sam Rockwell. Also featured in a small cameo role is George (as "Jerzy").

The film premiered in the U.S. on 30 September 2002 and went on to a limited theatrical release the following week. Against an estimated $13 million budget, it ended up grossing a paltry $75,000 over its opening weekend and ended up grossing $333,000. It fared better at European cinemas, particularly in the U.K., but was still, like *Rock Star*, a flop by any Hollywood standards.

Before either *Rock Star* or *Welcome to Collinwood* had made their inauspicous debuts, George reached a major milestone in August 2001 - his fortieth birthday. Michelle Pfeiffer and Nicole Kidman, who had each bet him $10,000 that he would be married by forty, had to admit defeat and send him their cheques. He returned both with the same note saying, "double or nothing", resetting the age deadline as fifty.

$112 million in the U.S. and a further $38 million worldwide, against a $35 million budget, it seemed that anything associated with George Clooney was now guaranteed success.

The *Ocean's Eleven* shoot wrapped on 7 June 2001. Instead of resting, George focused on producing. First up, a cinema release for a Maysville production, *Rock Star*, starring Mark Wahlberg and Jennifer Aniston.

The film, directed by Stephen Herek and written by John Stockwell, is about

7

THE DIRECTOR'S CHAIR

Ocean's Eleven premiered in the U.S. on 5 December 2001 and went on general release two days later. The film was an astounding success. Over the opening weekend alone, *Ocean's Eleven* took $38 million – nearly half the estimated $85 million budget. Reviews were glowing. *Rolling Stone* said: "As for Clooney, his effortless star power is a thing of beauty." *The San Francisco Chronicle* focused on George, too: "We first see Clooney as a graying, scraggly-looking prisoner. A minute later, he's out of jail. His hair has been cut and dyed and he's breezing into a casino in a sharp sports jacket, looking like someone who ought to be in pictures. Just as it's a kick to see Cary Grant or Fred Astaire walk across a room, it's a singular pleasure of *Ocean's Eleven* just to watch Clooney move."

The blockbuster would go on to gross $183 million in the U.S. alone and take millions more worldwide. When the final balance sheets were in, the film had grossed over $450 million. For a cast acting for a small fee against future profits, the share of profits was immense. For Soderbergh, George and Section Eight, the success of the film made them the toast of Hollywood.

Not content with jumping from being the biggest star in TV to being one of the biggest film actors in Hollywood, George then turned his attentions to a new challenge – directing. He has said that he had no specific ambitions to direct, that instead he simply found himself in a position where he either directed a film or it would never get made.

The film was *Confessions of a Dangerous Mind*. Various directors had been connected to the project, including Bryan Singer and David Fincher and just as many actors, including Johnny Depp and Russell Crowe, but nobody ever quite felt strongly enough about the film to sign on the dotted line. Signed to play a minor role, but not feeling as though he was suited to any of the lead parts, George had the idea to direct the film.

Once he made that commitment and brought on board Charlie Kaufman (then white hot for having written *Being John Malkovich*) to write the screenplay, George was inundated with calls from people wanting to be involved. He asked Julia Roberts and Drew Barrymore to join the project. They said yes and agreed to work for a reduced salary. Despite this, studios were reluctant to back the film as it seemed unlikely to be a moneyspinner. Conversely, independent producers were wary of the film, for fear that it would cost too much to make. Determined to make it happen, George made a passionate pitch to Miramax.

Having assured Miramax he could make it for less than $30 million, George won backing and brought it in for $27 million. The film was based on the autobiography of TV game show presenter, Chuck Barris, who claimed in the book that he had led a secret double life as a CIA agent. George felt a connection to the game show element of the story, having, of course, grown up with a father who had hosted a game show on TV. The other elements of the story spoke to his ongoing struggle to accept his celebrity. "I certainly had an understanding of fame and some of those trappings and of waking up and having

Previous spread: George shares an intimate moment with Natascha McElhone in *Solaris*.
Right: Drew Barrymore and Sam Rockwell with Director Clooney in *Confessions of a Dangerous Mind*.

other people's perceptions of you being much different from your own perception. So, the reason I felt that I could direct, was that I felt this was a screenplay I knew how to tell the story of."

The shoot started on 14 January 2002 and flowed smoothly. George had every scene storyboarded. He had fought for the actor Sam Rockwell to star in the film as "Chuck Barris" and Rockwell repaid George's belief in him, with a dazzling performance. For inspiration while shooting, George read Sidney Lumet's book on directing. The shoot wrapped on 17 April 2002.

No sooner had filming finished, than George was scheduled to start work on the new Steven Soderbergh film, which Section Eight would co-produce. Following *Ocean's Eleven*, Soderbergh had announced his intention to remake *Solaris*, a 1972 film by Andrei Tarkovsky based on a science fiction novel by Stanislaw Lem.

Soderbergh had not thought of casting George until George sent his Section Eight partner a letter asking that he consider him. "It's a film about questioning God and questioning relationships," he told *The Chicago Sun Times*, "which seemed different and exciting to me. I love to write people letters because it's an easy way to communicate, so I wrote Steven Soderbergh about why I wanted to do this project which is that I'm a guy who questions everything, too."

Soderbergh cast George as "Chris Kelvin", a psychiatrist sent to a space station circling the planet Solaris where two astronauts have committed suicide. He later told *The San Francisco Chronicle*: "*Solaris* required a complete dispersal of all the charm and good spirits that we normally associate with George. The other thing is, it's really a non-verbal part. It's a completely interior performance, like a lot of the great performances that George and

Above: George took only a minor role in *Confessions of a Dangerous Mind*, but also shouldered the task of directing.

I both enjoy from the American new wave films of the late sixties and early seventies. I thought of this as George's *Five Easy Pieces*."

George came off the *Confessions* shoot and arrived on set, ready to start working on *Solaris*. He was exhausted and wearing two hats: that of an actor about to start filming a part and that of a director who now needed to get hours of footage into the shape of a rough cut. George answered time restrictions by all but moving onto the Warner Bros lot. Most nights he slept in his trailer, which enabled him to work on both projects simultaneously. Within five weeks, he had a first cut of *Confessions*. By then, as he relayed to *USA Today*, he was practically sleepwalking in a parallel reality, "I had a golf cart right next to the trailer and I would come out in a spacesuit, exhausted and then jump into the cart and go edit my film during lunch and at night and in the morning before we shot. I slept at the office a bunch. I slept in my trailer. It was literally 17, 18, 19 hour days, every day. It was the hardest I've ever worked. I looked beat but I figured, 'What the hell if I look beat up and old? That's OK for the part of a tormented widower in *Solaris*.'"

In *Solaris*, the first night Chris Kelvin is at the space station, he wakes up and his wife, (played by Natasha McElhone) is in bed with him. This shocks him, since she committed suicide, back on earth, some time before. This replicant becomes what Kelvin remembers of his dead wife. Focussing on a theme of identity, the film is a far cry from anything else George had ever appeared in before. Critics like Roger Ebert later noted this determined move away from the public's perception of George: "Clooney has successfully survived being named *People* magazine's "Sexiest Man Alive" by deliberately choosing projects that ignore that image. His alliance with Soderbergh, both as an actor and co-producer, shows a taste for challenge. Here, as Kelvin, he is intelligent, withdrawn, sad, puzzled."

Despite his workload, George still managed to bring his trademark pranks and good humour to the set, as female lead McElhone, recalled: "George's always fooling around and making everyone laugh and putting everyone before himself, which is quite unactorly and certainly very unstarry."

One day in May 2002, while shooting a difficult scene, George received news that his Aunt Rosemary was dying. He went over to her house to say his goodbyes. He told her that he had just edited *Confessions* so the film played out to the sounds of her singing "There's No Business Like Showbusiness". She was apparently delighted and honoured. When she finally succumbed to lung cancer on 29 June 2002, George was devastated. At her funeral, he served as a pallbearer. Her death hung over the rest of the *Solaris* shoot. Filming, however, was mercifully short, lasting a total of only 43 days before wrapping in July 2002.

Four days later, George was on set for the first day of work on *Intolerable Cruelty*. For this latest Coen Brothers film, his paycheque was estimated at a staggering $15 million. It was time to put money in the bank after taking a nominal fee for *Confessions of a Dangerous Mind* and *Solaris*. After two integrity projects back to back, it was time to wheel out the other George, the mainstream, mass-market George. While *Solaris* and

Left: George was working up to 19 hours a day while filming *Solaris*.
Above: George's wedding day...with Catherine Zeta Jones in *Intolerable Cruelty*.

Confessions of a Dangerous Mind brought him critical kudos and respect as both an actor and a director, neither would endear him to the studio bosses, who sat hunched over calculators and flow charts, graphing bankability.

Intolerable Cruelty was a screwball comedy. Based on a story by Robert Ramsey, Matthew Stone and John Romano, the Coen Brothers had crafted a screenplay in collaboration with Ramsey and Stone. The story concerns "Marilyn Rexroth" (played by Catherine Zeta Jones) a golddigger who seemingly seduces rich men into marrying her, so that she can assume their wealth. She meets her match when her real estate developer husband seeks the help of "Miles Massey" (played by George), a noted Los Angeles divorce lawyer. Although at first he's ruthlessly suspicious of her, a few manipulations on her part change his mind and slowly he finds himself recasting his thoughts on her and, in doing so, falls hard for her. Shooting on the film wrapped in September 2002, at which time George came off a whirlwind three projects, all shot back-to-back.

He took a much-needed break and headed to Italy on holiday. There, a stunning property on the edge of Lake Como caught his eye. Finding it for sale, he bought the 18th century Villa Oleandra, which has 15 bedrooms, for an estimated $7 million. The vendors, according to ABC news, were the Heinz family. Three years later, he also acquired the adjoining Villa Margherita, also dating back to the 18th century. Both are in the small village of Laglio.

Section Eight was gathering momentum with a further two co-productions underway. The first involved George serving as one of many executive producers on the feature film, *Far From Heaven*, starring Julianne Moore and directed by Todd Haynes. The acclaimed film would open in cinemas on 22 November 2002. Another, again with George in the executive producer role, was

Right: George's home, Villa Oleandra, on Lake Como in Italy.

the Al Pacino vehicle, *Insomnia*, directed by Christopher Nolan, which hit cinemas in the U.S. on 24 May 2002.

Despite originally having had a December release date on the schedule, *Solaris* premiered in the U.S. on 19 November 2002 and opened at cinemas in the U.S. on 27 November. Reviews were tepid and the film had a poor opening weekend, taking just under $7 million. Then, against its estimated budget of $47 million, it only went on to gross $14 million on home soil. It fared slightly better worldwide, taking $15 million.

George later blamed the box office performance on the way the film was marketed, telling *The Daily Telegraph*, "It's a polarising film. Fox agreed to make it but didn't commit to the idea of how to sell it. They sold it as a space film, which it isn't and I was in the trailer naked. The people who did see it hated it. So we were playing to the wrong audience, that's what." He was alluding to a scene in the film, in which his bare buttocks famously appear. A still from that scene was used as a promotional tool for the film – an image wildly misrepresentative of the film itself.

On 31 December 2002, *Confessions of a Dangerous Mind* opened at U.S. cinemas on limited release, before opening on general release on 24 January. The film ended up grossing $16 million on home soil and a further $17 million worldwide. In short, it was a modest commercial success, in light of the estimated $27 million budget. However, the film was a great critical success. *The Guardian* called it a "sprightly and entertaining picture". Roger Ebert, reviewing it for *The Chicago Sun Times*, summed up the film's plot as succinctly as ever, "Barris himself claims to have killed 33 times for the CIA. It's in his book. He had the perfect cover: The creator of 'The Dating Game' and 'The Gong Show' would accompany his lucky winners on trips to romantic spots such as Helsinki in midwinter and kill for the CIA while the winners regaled each other with reindeer steaks. Who, after all, would ever suspect him?"

"THEY SOLD IT AS A SPACE FILM, WHICH IT ISN'T AND I WAS IN THE TRAILER NAKED. THE PEOPLE WHO DID SEE IT HATED IT. SO WE WERE PLAYING TO THE WRONG AUDIENCE . . ."

Left: Despite its appearance, George insisted that it was wrong to market *Solaris* as a space movie.

Of George as director, Ebert said, "That this would be the first project to attract George Clooney as a director is not so surprising if you know that his father directed game shows, and he was often a backstage observer. That Clooney would direct it so well is a little surprising and is part of that re-education by which we stop thinking of Clooney as a TV hunk and realize he is smart and curious. His first movie is not only intriguing as a story but great to look at, a marriage of bright pop images from the 1960s and 1970s and dark, cold spyscapes that seem to have wandered in from John le Carré." George must have read that review and grinned – such validation and from one of the most influential American film critics.

Early in 2003, Section Eight were busy again, this time co-producing a TV show called *K Street*, with Sennet-Gernstein Entertainment. There was a personal twist here for George, which took him back to the past. Among the cast were, his ex-wife, Talia Balsam and her husband, actor John Slattery, whose credits at that point included *Will & Grace*, *Sex and the City*, *Party of Five* and many made-for-TV films. Revolving around the work and lives of political consultants, *K Street* featured Talia across four episodes, as "Gail". Fictional characters appeared alongside real life political consultants in the series which was shot on location in Washington D.C. Episodes were shot within the week of airing, to keep political relevance to an optimum. The show launched on HBO on 14 September 2003 and ran for ten episodes, each lasting thirty minutes. The finale of that one and only season aired 16 November. During the series' shoot lifetime, George ended up reconnecting with Talia, making peace with her over their past, as he told *Esquire*, "Her husband was a regular. It was really nice to reintroduce myself to her and relearn about her. Now we can look at ourselves as two people who had a reason to be together at a point in the past. We were able to get past

Right: *Confessions of a Dangerous Mind* made only minor profits but was a great critical success.

the rough times in the past, just make jokes and have fun."

As well as putting politics on TV, an increasingly political George was also busy fielding critiques of his personal politics in the media. Back in January 2003, he had expressed his fears on *The Charlie Rose Show* about the possibility of the U.S. invading Iraq. In the interview he said: "the government itself is running exactly like the Sopranos". He said he was concerned that the U.S. were going to "go into a war and kill a lot of innocent people" and believed that talks must be exhausted first: "Are we going to try and talk to Saddam Hussein . . . without jumping in and killing people first? I don't believe we're going to wait until the last resort to do it. That's what bothers me." The interview came at a time when artists such as Sean Penn were speaking out against a war with Iraq.

When the threat of invasion became reality in March 2003, George made his views public and, like other artists who did so, he became a focal point for Republican/patriotic anger. His father told him that he should be a man and accept

that speaking one's mind will attract equally candid critiques from the other side of the political spectrum.

In October 2003, George reflected on a year of such critiques to *The Age*, telling them, "I'm a liberal, big time: a famous liberal. I got picketed at Miramax and picketed at Universal because I came out against the war in February, but that's fine. I can take it. It probably hurt some things, but not so bad. And since it is now a world where it is hard to hear a dissenting voice, basically I was representing 50 per cent of the country. I still believe it's the dumbest thing we've done as a country and I still think the world is in upheaval because of it."

Premiering at the Venice Film Festival in September 2003, *Intolerable Cruelty* opened in the U.S. on 10 October. Against an estimated $60 million budget, the film grossed $35 million in the U.S., before going on to take a further $85 million worldwide.

Once again, as penance to "Commercial Hollywood" for the modest takings of *Solaris* and *Confessions of a Dangerous Mind*, George had attached his name to a mainstream blockbuster.

Left: George puts his point across in *Intolerable Cruelty* just as he was now doing in real life on the public stage. Above: George and Catherine Zeta Jones certainly had cause to celebrate when *Intolerable Cruelty* became an international blockbuster.

8

RENAISSANCE MAN

By late 2003, it was definite that Steven Soderbergh and George were going to make a sequel to *Ocean's Eleven*, called . . . *Ocean's Twelve*. The screenplay would be penned by George Nolfi, who had previously written the 2003 film, *Timeline*. After the colossal success of *Ocean's Eleven*, the headache was once again financing. How would they secure the same stellar cast, necessary to make the sequel work, in terms of what would surely now be colossal salary demands from the stars' agents?

oderbergh and George went back to Brad Pitt *et al* and pitched the sequel as follows: the film would be produced for the exact same budget as the first film and once more, the cast would work for salaries below their going rate. Everyone from the original signed up and the project was on. While on the publicity tour for the first film, Soderbergh had visited Rome for the first time and fallen in love with the city. Consequently, he told Nolfi that this time, he imagined the film's plot to be Euro-centric.

At the turn of 2004, Section Eight had two small films in co-production. The first, *Criminal*, directed by Gregory Jacobs, starred John C Reilly, Diego Luna and Maggie Gyllenhall and told the story of two con artists out to swindle a currency collector. That film premiered at the Seattle International Film Festival on 12 June 2004 and opened on a limited release on 24 October. The film grossed less than $1 million in the U.S. The second film, *The Jacket*, directed by John Maybury and starring Adrien Brody, Keira Knightley, Kris Kristoffersen and Jennifer Jason Leigh, concerned the psychological torments and inner journey of a Gulf War veteran. The film would later premiere at the Sundance Film Festival on 23 January 2005 and go on general release from March 2005. Against an estimated $29 million budget, the film grossed slightly over $20 million worldwide. Late in 1994, Section Eight also co-produced a short film, *The Big Empty*, directed by J. Lisa Chang and Newton Thomas Sigel. The twenty minute short, marketed as the "bittersweet tale of Alice, her vagina, and the infinite nature of the tundra", starred Selma Blair. It premiered at the Austin Film Festival in October 2005.

In early 2004, George's on/off relationship with Lisa Snowdon was reported to be on again. The couple were said to have reunited during the *Ocean's Twelve* shoot, which started in Rome in March 2004, moving on to Monaco, Paris, Amsterdam, Lake Como and Sicily, as well as various locations across the U.S.

Previous Spread: George as CIA agent "Bob Barnes" in *Syriana*.
Below: George put on 38 lbs (17.2 kg) in weight for the *Syriana* role.
Right: With Matt Damon and Brad Pitt in Amsterdam on *Ocean's Twleve*.

Alongside the original cast, new faces were added to up the star power – Catherine Zeta Jones as Europol investigator "Isabel Lahiri", Vincent Cassel as ace thief "The Night Fox", Eddie Izzard as "Roman Nagel" and even Bruce Willis… playing himself.

The plot picks up where *Ocean's Eleven* left off. Having successfully cleaned out Terry Benedict's $160 million casino fortune in the first film, the team have since been dormant, each enjoying his share of the bounty. In the new film, Benedict has discovered the identity of Ocean's Eleven and wants his money back in two weeks with interest – or else.

The film quickly establishes the whereabouts of Ocean's Eleven. Danny Ocean has remarried "Tess" (Julia Roberts) and is living a quiet life in Connecticut. Faced with Benedict's ultimatum, which could slap them all back in jail and, having blown most of the money, Danny has to reassemble Ocean's Eleven and head for Europe, where they believe they can pull off jobs that will yield the kind of cash needed to pay off Benedict's threat. There, they hook up with the Night Fox and plan a daring heist in Rome.

The shoot wrapped on 12 July 2004. In typical George fashion, he had barely come off the *Ocean's Twelve* shoot before it was time to race into preparation for his next role in *Syriana*. The political thriller, set amidst the global oil industry, was written and slated to be directed by Stephen Gaghan, who had previously written and directed *Abandon*, a 2002 film starring Katie Holmes. He was best known as the screenwriter of Soderbergh's and employed a similarly ambitious multiple storyline plot structure for *Syriana*. The screenplay was inspired by former CIA agent, Robert Baer's memoir, *See No Evil*, which Soderbergh and George both read and then lent to Gaghan. The book chronicles Baer's missions and operations in the Middle East between 1976 and 1997.

George was to play CIA operative

"Bob Barnes", a man close to retiring after a long and respectable career, offered one last mission. With the U.S. still occupying Iraq, the film had guaranteed political resonance. But for this reason, it was sure to struggle to find studio backing. Therefore, to help get the film off the ground, George cut his paycheque to $350,000. As with so many releases on his CV from this era, the film was co-produced by Section Eight, George and Soderbergh serving as Executive Producers.

The film started shooting that August, with an estimated $50 million budget in place. In the small window of time between finishing work on *Ocean's Twelve* and starting work on *Syriana*, George needed radically to alter his appearance to play Bob Barnes with conviction. To achieve this, he shaved his hairline back and grew a beard. Installed at his Lake Como house, he ate fine Italian food around the clock, up to eight meals a day, until he had gained 38 lbs (17.2 kg). By the time he had fattened up, the film was ready to shoot, complete with Matt Damon on board and a cameo role secured for William Hurt.

Filming took place on location throughout the U.S., as well as in more exotic locations like Dubai, Geneva, Egypt and Casablanca, which doubled up for the primary locations in the film: Tehran and Beirut.

During one scene, in which Barnes is tied to a chair and tortured, the chair was

Previous spread:
Syriana was to be a huge commercial and critical success for George.
Left: George with Julia Roberts in *Ocean's Twelve*, not as successful as its predecessor, but still a huge earner at the box office.

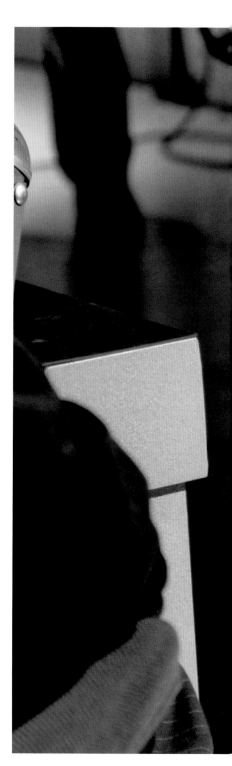

kicked too hard and George went flying back. His hands tied, he could do nothing to stop the speed with which the chair toppled over. His head walloped against the floor. Initially, he was a little shocked, but there seemed to be no injury. By the time the film wrapped in November, however, he was suffering excruciating headaches and experiencing pockets of short term memory loss.

The ill health that plagued him over the coming months led him to tell *The Sunday Times* in October 2005, that he'd just come out of "the worst year I've ever had". The accident while filming *Syriana*, had, unbenownst to George, torn his dura mater, the tough layering which wraps the spinal cord and brain. At first, doctors did not know what was causing the headaches, which George likened to a constant severe ice cream headache. Then spinal fluid began leaking from his nose. At that time, a correct diagnosis was made. Surgery was immediately scheduled. After that, the pain subsided. The relief was stupendous, as George recalled, "Before the surgery it was the most unbearable pain I've ever been through, literally where you'd go, 'Well, you'll have to kill yourself at some point. You can't live like this.'" He later said he had not actually experienced any suicidal thoughts. It was to be some time before he would finally be free of the pain and the lapses of memory.

The illness was just one calamity in his life that year. His sister Ada's husband died suddenly at the age of 45 of a heart attack and his grandmother broke her hip and died. To complete a year of tragedy, George's beloved dog also died, attacked and killed by a rattlesnake.

On 10 December 2004, *Ocean's Twelve* opened at cinemas. Against a budget that ended up being somewhere close to $110 million, the film grossed $326 million worldwide – nearly $120 million less than Ocean's Eleven. Reviews were outright critical. *The Guardian* pronounced it a, "horrifically smug and disappointing sequel", while *Rolling Stone* complained,

Right: As well as directing and appearing in *Good Night and Good Luck*, George co-wrote the screenplay with his friend Grant Heslov.

"It's not enough to watch privileged stars, including Julia Roberts and newbie Catherine Zeta-Jones as a Europol cop, enjoying their privileges. It has to look like the whole thing rolled off their backs. Clooney and company work it too hard this time. You can tell they're huffing and puffing to stay afloat."

Prior to the film hitting cinemas, George was in agony and had no choice but to cancel elements of the *Ocean's Twelve* publicity schedule. The story going around was that he had ruptured a disc in his back – that it was a combination of the torture scene accident and George's exercise regimen once the film wrapped, which was designed rapidly to shed the excess weight he had gained for the part. No one realised at the time that George was suffering from the torn dura mater, a condition that can cause paralysis or even death.

On 9 January 2005, a new TV show made its debut on HBO. It was called *Unscripted* and starred Krista Allen, who had appeared in *Confessions of a Dangerous Mind*. The show which, as the title suggests, was improvised, ran for one season. The last of ten episodes,

aired on 27 February 2005. The show was a co-production between Section Eight/Warner Bros and HBO, revolving around a group of actors and actresses trying to make it in Los Angeles. The cast appeared as themselves in the fictional story, Krista Allen, for example, playing a character called "Krista Allen". George himself directed the first five episodes of the show, Grant Heslov directed the second five. Reviews leaned towards describing the show as too insiderish to have mainstream appeal.

Next, George and Section Eight, in a co-production, began work on *Good Night And Good Luck*, George's second outing as a director. Unlike *Confessions of a Dangerous Mind*, for which George had valiantly settled into the director's chair out of necessity, this time George was most definitely out to direct. He co-wrote the screenplay with close friend Grant Heslov and beyond that, intended to produce, direct the film and even act in it, too, as "Fred Friendly".

The film told the story of broadcast journalist Edward R. Murrow (George's father's boyhood hero) who fearlessly took on all kinds of political giants, most

"ALL MY LIFE I HAVE BEEN FASCINATED WITH
THE THREE GREAT MOMENTS IN AMERICAN
JOURNALISM: MURROW TAKING ON McCARTHY;
CRONKITE POINTING TO A MAP OF VIETNAM
AND SAYING, 'THIS IS A MISTAKE'; WOODWARD
AND BERNSTEIN EXPOSING WATERGATE."

notoriously Senator Joseph McCarthy. His equally famous producer was Fred Friendly. Instead of billing itself as a biopic, the film instead centred on Murrow's determined bid to unmask McCarthy's bullying politics.

For George, the film had two inspirations: it took him back to when he was growing up in a politically liberal family with a father who worked in broadcast journalism; it also chimed with the recent witchhunt he'd felt caught up in after coming out in criticism of the American government and the U.S. invasion of Iraq.

George explained his passion for the project to *The Times*, "All my life, I have been fascinated with what are probably the great three moments in American journalism: Murrow taking on McCarthy; Walter Cronkite stepping from behind his desk, pointing to the map of Vietnam and saying, 'This is a mistake'; Woodward and Bernstein exposing Watergate."

The film started shooting in February 2005. It was shot in black and white, to capture the era. The budget was roughly $7.5 million. To cut costs, George agreed to pay himself $1 for directing and $1 for co-writing the screenplay. That way, most of the film's budget would go to production.

To play "Edward R Murrow", he cast David Strathairn, who was born in San Francisco in 1949 and had appeared in many films and TV shows, notably *A League of Their Own*, *Bob Roberts*, *The Firm* and *Passion Fish*.

Deciding that nobody could possibly render McCarthy as he actually was, George made the decision to use archive footage of the senator. The shoot wrapped in April 2005.

In June, reports emerged that George and Lisa Snowdon's on/off relationship

had officially ended. The issues cited were Snowdon's reluctance to leave her home in the U.K. and move to Los Angeles and George's incessant work schedule. Between work and geography, the couple had constantly been battling the problems of a long distance relationship.

There was no time to think of the break-up as Section Eight geared up to start production on *The Good German*, the latest Clooney/Soderbergh feature. Soderbergh was directing, with George playing "Jake Geismer". The screenplay was by Paul Attanasio, who had previously worked on *Disclosure* and *Donnie Brasco*, based on the novel, *The Good German*, by Joseph Kanon.

The story is set in Berlin in 1945, in the aftermath of the Second World War. As the Allied powers fight over control of the city, an American war correspondent, Jake Geismer, returns for a visit. As he walks through the rubble, his mind is less on the politics than on the German woman he last saw in the 1930s. He manages to track down "Lena" (Cate Blanchett) but to his dismay, she has been forced into prostitution. Then events happen which jeopardise Geismer's reputation and cast suspicion over Lena's recent past.

With Tobey Maguire in place as supporting actor, *The Good German* started shooting on 27 September 2005 on soundstages in California, armed with a $32 million budget. Like *Good Night And Good Luck*, Soderbergh shot the film in black and white. The shoot wrapped before the end of the year.

Meanwhile, *Good Night And Good Luck* premiered at the Venice Film Festival on 1 September 2005, before opening at U.S. cinemas on 14 October. Reviews were positive. *Rolling Stone* theorised, "You have to wonder why the star of *Ocean's Eleven* would risk his standing as a pinup . . . to direct, co-write and co-star in a movie set in the 1950s, shot in black-and-white and focused on a fifty year old battle between TV newsman Edward R. Murrow, indelibly played by David Strathairn and the Commie-hunting Sen. Joseph McCarthy",

Right: Shot in black and white, *The Good German* was set in Berlin in 1945 , immediately following the end of the Second World War.

George
CLOONEY · Caté **BLANCHETT** · Tobey **MAGUIRE**

The **Good German**

IF WAR IS HELL
THEN WHAT COMES AFTER?

WARNER BROS. PICTURES PRESENTS
IN ASSOCIATION WITH VIRTUAL STUDIOS A SECTION EIGHT PRODUCTION GEORGE CLOONEY CATE BLANCHETT TOBEY MAGUIRE
THE GOOD GERMAN MUSIC BY THOMAS NEWMAN CASTING BY DEBRA ZANE C.S.A. COSTUME DESIGNER LOUISE FROGLEY PRODUCTION DESIGNER PHILIP MESSINA
BASED ON THE NOVEL BY JOSEPH KANON EXECUTIVE PRODUCERS BENJAMIN WAISBREN FREDERIC W. BROST PRODUCED BY BEN COSGROVE GREGORY JACOBS SCREENPLAY BY PAUL ATTANASIO
DIRECTED BY STEVEN SODERBERGH WARNER BROS. PICTURES

R RESTRICTED
UNDER 17 REQUIRES ACCOMPANYING PARENT OR ADULT GUARDIAN
LANGUAGE, VIOLENCE AND SOME SEXUAL CONTENT
www.thegoodgerman.com

In Theaters Soon

before passing a warm verdict: "As a director, Clooney moves with admirable speed and economy. He sometimes tripped over his ambitions in *Confessions of a Dangerous Mind*, his 2002 debut behind the camera. But here his hand is assured, his wit focused, his target never in doubt."

The Observer also enthused about George's blooming capabilities, "Clooney's excellent film uses the past to make today's media and their audiences address their responsibilities in the way that, back in 1953, Arthur Miller's *The Crucible* drew on the Salem witch trials to make his fellow Americans face up to McCarthyism."

The film grossed $31 million on home soil, before going on to gross a further $23 million worldwide – providing an excellent return on its modest budget. The film would also go on to reap an impressive number of award nominations and wins. There would be six Academy Award nominations in 2006, across various categories: "Best Achievement in Art Direction", "Best Achievement in Cinematography", "Best Achievement in Directing", "Best Motion Picture of the Year", "Best Performance by an Actor in a Leading Role", "Best Writing Original Screenplay". The film won no actual Oscars, but the recognition was colossal.

In the U.K., the film picked up six BAFTA nominations: "Best Editing", "Best Film", "Best Performance by an Actor in a Leading Role", "Best Performance by an Actor in a Supporting Role", "Best Screenplay – Original" and "The David Lean Award for Direction". Again, no wins, but an amazing array of nominations.

There were also four Golden Globe nominations: "Best Director Motion Picture", "Best Motion Picture Drama", "Best Screenplay Motion Picture" and "Best Performance by an Actor in a Motion Picture – Drama".

At the Independent Spirit awards, the film won the "Best Cinematography" prize and picked up nominations for "Best Director", "Best Feature" and "Best Male Lead". The film also fared well at

Right: As well as making money at the box office, *Good Night and Good Luck* picked up a raft of awards nominations.

Above: An accident while filming a torture scene in *Syriana* left George with a brain injury that could have killed him.

the Venice Film Festival in 2005, where George must have been delighted to receive the "Human Rights Film Network Award - Special Mention". The screenplay was also nominated for the Writers' Guild of America Award (Screen) for "Best Original Screenplay". There were many other nominations to add to this already extraordinary round. If George had any nagging doubts about his potential future

as a director, should that be the path he chose to take, then this must have silenced them completely.

Also during 2005, George signed a deal to supply a voiceover for TV and radio advertisements for Budweiser beer. Although he had signed up for commercials advertising Martini and Fiat outside the U.S. before, this would be the first time his advertisement work would appear in the

American market. A year earlier, Fiat had hired George for a European ad campaign, designed to sell more Fiat cars to female drivers. Both campaigns joined the list of other products he had advertised, such as Martini and Nescafe.

George had also been producing again. Section Eight had co-produced *Rumor Has It*, which would open on 22 December 2005. The film, directed by Rob Reiner and written by Ted Griffin, starred Jennifer Aniston as "Sarah Huttinger", a woman who hears a rumour that her family was the inspiration for the book and film, *The Graduate*.

George served as Executive Producer on the film, which grossed $82 million worldwide. By the time *Rumor Has It* was at the cinemas, Section Eight was already gearing up to co-produce Richard Linklater's new animated film, *A Scanner Darkly*, an adaptation of the Philip K. Dick novel, which would open at U.S. cinemas on 28 July 2006 and gross $7 million worldwide.

On 9 December 2005, *Syriana* opened in U.S. cinemas. Against its $50 million budget, the film ended up grossing a healthy $93 worldwide. Reviews were strong. *Variety* said, "Those complaining that Hollywood never turns out films of topical or political substance are likely to embrace *Syriana*, a weighty and deeply intriguing look at the many tentacled beast that is the international oil industry"; while *The Los Angeles Times* called it, "conspiracy-theory filmmaking of the most bravura kind." *USA Today* specifically praised George saying, "Clooney does a masterful job portraying a smart guy who knows he should probably take a desk job in D.C., but is hooked on the adrenaline rush of top secret overseas assignments."

The film would go on to collect two Academy Award nominations, a BAFTA nomination for "Best Performance by an Actor in a Supporting Role", a Screen Actors Guild nomination for "Outstanding Performance by a Male Actor in a Supporting Role" and two Golden Globes nominations for "Best Original Score – Motion Picture".

Although 2005 turned out to be a year in which George's professional life had hit the kind of highs that he had long dreamed it would, in his personal life he had experienced twelve hard months of pain and sorrow.

Above right: *Good Night and Good Luck* was seen as a public awakening of George's political sensibilities.

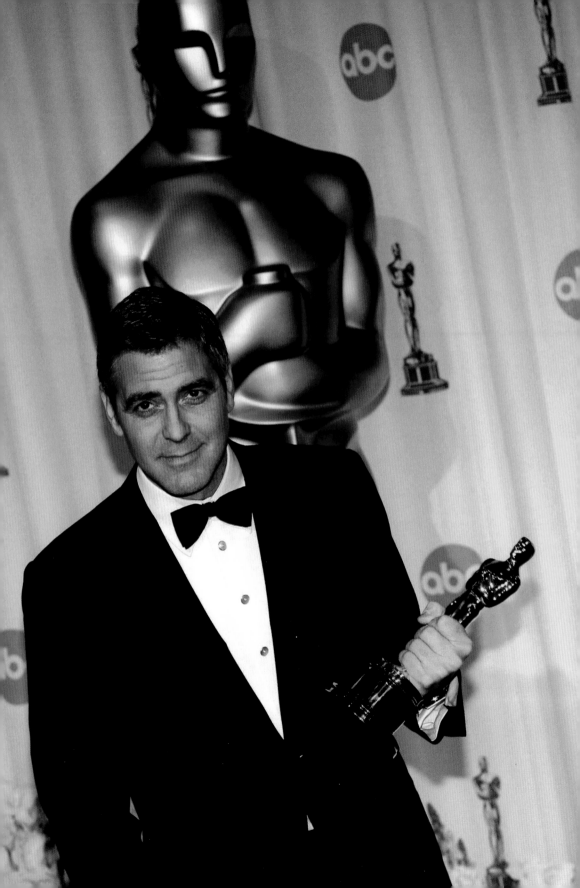

9

THE FANTASTIC
MR CLOONEY

And then it came, a lovely blast of Hollywood recognition. On the night of

16 January 2006, at the Golden Globe awards, George was attending in

support of nominations for both *Good Night And Good Luck* and *Syriana*.

Good Night And Good Luck ended up losing out on the "Best Director"

award to Ang Lee for *Brokeback Mountain*. It also lost out on "Best Original

Screenplay" to *Brokeback Mountain*. Ditto "Best Motion Picture Drama".

But that night, George did win the award for "Best Performance by an

Actor in a Supporting Role in a Motion Picture" for his work on *Syriana*.

N ever one to stop working for long, George was hard at work on the shoot for *Michael Clayton*, one of the latest projects Section Eight were co-producing. Written and directed by Tony Gilroy, who had written the screenplay for twin blockbusters, *The Bourne Identity* and *The Bourne Supremacy*, *Michael Clayton* was slated to be a legal thriller. The film would star George in the title role and Tom Wilkinson as "Arthur Edens". It was to have a budget of $25 million.

The film told the story of "Michael Clayton", an in house fixer for a powerful New York law firm headed up by Sydney Pollack. There's a problem – one of the top partners, "Arthur Edens", has cracked up, and it's up to Clayton, down on his luck himself, to make the bad smell go away.

George was unsure about taking the part at first, but Soderbergh convinced him he was right for the role. He arrived on the shoot, exhausted, straight from working on *The Good German*, ready to act opposite Tom Wilkinson and Tilda Swinton.

Mid production, on 5 March 2006, at the 78th Academy Awards ceremony, George was once more in the audience, the nervous parent of two films. First up, he was there because *Good Night And Good Luck* had been nominated for those six glorious awards and second, because *Syriana* had also collected two nominations, for "Best Writing – Original Screenplay" and "Best Performance by an Actor in a Supporting Role". Personally, he was up for "Best Achievement In Directing", "Best Performance by an Actor in a Supporting Role" and "Best Writing – Original Screenplay". That night, in a repeat of what happened at the Golden Globes, George won the "Best Performance by an

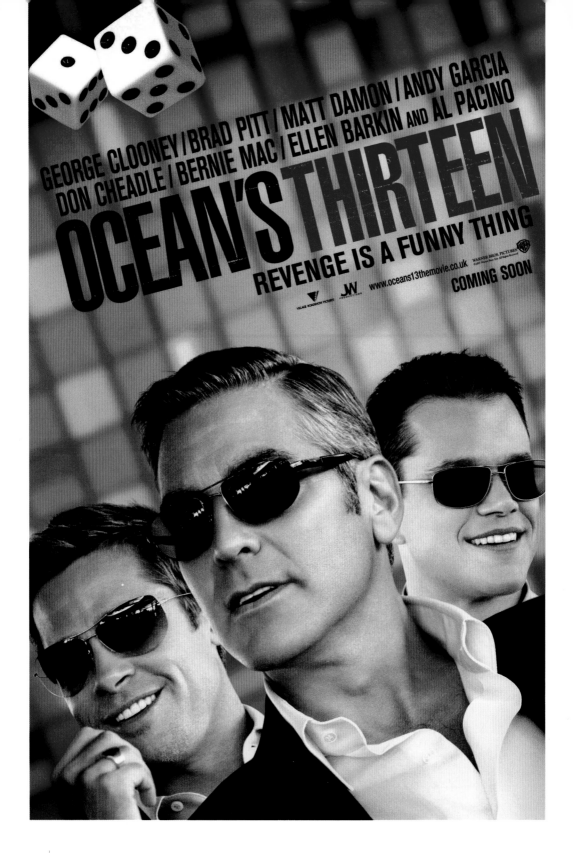

Actor in a Supporting Role" for his work on *Syriana*, but lost out in the other categories.

Michael Clayton wrapped in early April 2006 and George immediately turned his attentions to global politics. He and his journalist father, Nick, flew out to Eastern Chad and Southern Sudan, to visit the people of the turbulent Darfur region. In doing so, they hoped to draw international attention to the ever-escalating humanitarian crisis.

Once there, George told reporters he had made the journey to try to help show the truth down on the ground, to beam the news back to Americans at home that they needed to help. He could not sit, indifferent, in Los Angeles, when 200,000 had died and a further 2.5 million had been displaced.

Consequently, he was prepared to do whatever it might take to put an end to the violence and the suffering. When asked why, as a movie star, he was there, he said he felt it was his duty to use "the credit card that you get for being famous

Left: Al Pacino and Ellen Barkin joined in the fun when shooting began on *Ocean's Thirteen* in July 2006.
Below: George put his weight behind the environmental movement when he placed an order for a new "green" car in August 2006.

Above: George with Don Cheadle meeting the Egyptian Foreign Minister Ahmed Abul Gheit in Cairo in December 2006, campaigning for famine relief in Darfur.

Right: George was named as a United Nations Messenger for Peace at the UN in New York in January 2008.

in the right instances whenever you can."

Ever thinking of the moving image, George and his father filmed their trip, which eventually became the half-hour documentary, *A Journey To Darfur*. It would later premiere on the AmericanLife TV network on 15 January 2007.

Not everyone agreed with George taking to the world political stage in the tradition of Marlon Brando, Sean Penn, Tim Robbins, Jane Fonda, Susan Sarandon, Robert Redford and Bono. *The Guardian* criticised the trip, making much of what they perceived to be inconsistencies between the 45-year-old's avid opposition to the U.S. military invasion of Iraq and his calling for U.N. military intervention in Darfur. "Not long ago he was the pin-up boy for

the Bring Our Boys Home From Iraq lobby; now he is the pin-up leader of the Save Darfur campaign. He is pretty much the pretty-boy mouthpiece for U.S. imperialism, for the idea that it is up to the likes of America and the international community to resolve Africa's crises."

On 21 July 2006, *Ocean's Thirteen* started shooting. Soderbergh had already envisaged the second sequel as he finished work on *Ocean's Twelve*. It had suddenly dawned on him that the team should return to Las Vegas for one last sequel. Producer Jerry Weintraub rounded up everyone involved in the budding franchise and warned them that in summer 2006, they would need to be free to complete the trilogy.

This time, the story starts with

"Reuben Tishkoff" (Elliott Giould) back in Las Vegas, where he's got himself stuck in a rocky partnership with "Willy Bank" (played by Al Pacino). When the partnership sours, Reuben realises that his old friends and colleagues, notably "Danny Ocean", were right in warning him against such an alliance. With their friend in trouble, Danny Ocean makes a few calls and assembles the old gang to help Reuben by taking down Willy Bank's casino – the richest in the world.

As before, they worked to an $85 million budget and everybody signed up for a cut of the profits. Shot on location in Nevada and California, to a script this time by Brian Koppelman and David Levien, the film featured neither Julia Roberts nor Catherine Zeta Jones. In the female lead this time, was Ellen Barkin, playing "Abigail Sponder", Banks' hotel manageress.

On 1 August 2006, Section Eight officially ceased to take on new projects. George and Soderbergh were going their separate ways. The split was simply down to Soderbergh wanting to concentrate his energies on filmmaking and withdraw from being so busy with production and development.

George, on the other hand, wanted to carry on multitasking. The very same day Section Eight made that announcement, George launched a new production company, once more under the Warner Bros umbrella, called Smoke House. This would be co-run with his close friend, Grant Heslov, who had been looking after Section Eight's TV operations since its inception.

In the meantime, Section Eight would remain operational, until its schedule was cleared – which meant getting *Ocean's Thirteen*, *Wind Chill*, a made-for-TV film called *The Half Life of Timofey Berezin* and *Michael Clayton* to completion. At that point, Soderbergh and George would no longer be active under the name of Section Eight

That August, George placed an order

Right: George behind the camera in his role as Director on *Leatherheads*.

"WE WERE BROUGHT UP TO BELIEVE THAT THE U.N. WAS FORMED TO ENSURE THAT THE HOLOCAUST COULD NEVER HAPPEN AGAIN ... HOW YOU DEAL WITH IT [DARFUR] WILL BE YOUR LEGACY – YOUR RWANDA, YOUR CAMBODIA, YOUR AUSCHWITZ."

for one of the first limited edition electric cars to be made by Tesla Motors. He managed to put his name down for one of only a hundred of the environmentally friendly vehicles, now apparently also lending his public persona to environmental issues.

In September 2006, an impassioned George stood before the U.N. and gave a rousing speech to the Security Council about the humanitarian crisis in Darfur, calling for U.N. sanctions and an on-the-ground intervention by a peacekeeping force to prevent further atrocities.

"We were brought up to believe that the U.N. was formed to ensure that the Holocaust could never happen again," Clooney told the council, "so after September 30, you won't need the U.N. You will simply need men with shovels and bleached white linen and headstones. How you deal with it will be your legacy – your Rwanda, your Cambodia, your Auschwitz."

In November 2006, for a second time, *People* magazine named George the "Sexiest Man Alive". This time around, the award sat rather more awkwardly with a man who was developing such a serious public reputation.

That December, he took his campaign to Egypt, where he met members of the government in Cairo in a bid to persuade them to assist and protect the 2.5 million citizens displaced by the fighting. A week earlier, George had carried the same plea and message to the Chinese Government, one of Sudan's biggest oil customers.

George tried to persuade the Chinese, who had not endorsed U.N. demands that Sudan accept a U.N.

peacekeeping force, to change their minds and allow the African Union's 7,000-strong force in the country, to be replaced by a much larger U.N. contingent. By all accounts, he received a warmer and more receptive welcome in Cairo, than he did in Beijing, where the handshake was reportedly frosty.

The mission complete, George went back to the U.S., where he had to bury Max, his beloved Vietnamese pot bellied pig, who died on 1 December, after eighteen years of companionship.

George had little time to dwell on Max's death, however, as *The Good German* opened at cinemas, on 22 December 2006. Against the $32 million budget, in the all-important U.S. market, the film grossed $1.2 million – an unheard of flop for a Soderbergh/Clooney collaboration. Worldwide, it drew a healthier $4 million, but overall it was a commercial catastrophe.

The film was not helped by lukewarm reviews. *The Guardian* was scathing, writing: "Director Steven Soderbergh and his leading man, George Clooney, have cooked up a monumentally misjudged, self-regarding and emptily cynical take on 1940s thrillers in general and *Casablanca* in particular, by making a glossy pastiche noir set in the shattered ruins of 1945 Berlin."

The Village Voice summarised: "If *Casablanca* was the acme of wartime romanticism, *The Good German* is its self-conscious antithesis. Soderbergh wants to show the birth of post-war moral relativism. It's hard to believe in anything—his characters most of all."

To end the year, George was given the coveted American Cinematheque award at the end of 2006, a prize which recognised the tremendous calibre of his work across all sectors of the entertainment business.

2007 rolled into view with George preparing to shoot *Leatherheads*, the film he had been considering making for several years. A Smoke House co-

Previous spread: Renee Zellweger starred with George in the offbeat American football comedy *Leatherheads*.
Right: George with Sarah Larson at the *Leatherheads* premiere in Los Angeles in March 2008. The couple were to split within two months.

production, it was George's first project post-Section Eight.

He had previously talked about it as a 1920s screwball comedy about American football and at one point, Soderbergh was going to direct and George was going to star in it. Now, he was directing, producing and even starring in the film as "Dodge Connolly", opposite Renee Zwellweger, as "Lexie Littleton".

Written by Duncan Brantley and Rick Reilly, the film is set in 1925 and sees George play the captain of an ailing football team, who woos a college star to his team in the hope of turning around their fortunes. Into the mix, comes Lexie, love interest, a reporter, for whom Dodge falls. The shoot started on 12 February 2007 and wrapped on 17 May. All locations were in the Southern U.S.

Mid filming, George co-founded a non-profit organisation called Not On Our Watch, whose intention was to highlight atrocities taking place in the world. The first goal was to bring as much global attention as possible to the crisis in Darfur and attempt to bring about a peaceful resolution.

In June, *Ocean's Thirteen* became another huge success, even if reviews were, once again, mixed. Roger Ebert wrote in *The Chicago Sun Times*; "*Ocean's Thirteen* proceeds with insouciant dialogue, studied casualness and a lotta stuff happening, none of which I cared much about because the movie doesn't pause to develop the characters, who are forced to make do with their movie-star personas."

Variety disagreed, saying; "*Ocean's Thirteen* continues the breezy good times of the first two series entries without missing a beat." At the box office, the film grossed $36 million over its opening weekend in the U.S. alone and went on to gross $311 million worldwide – the lowest-ranking of the three films. Despite this, by any Hollywood standard, the film still turned a tremendous profit.

After the premiere in Las Vegas, at a

Right: George was nominated for an Academy Award for his performance in *Michael Clayton*.

cast party, George met a cocktail waitress at the Palms Casino resort. Her name was Sarah Larson. She was 28 and had once been a contestant on the game show, *Fear Factor*. They clicked and started going out. That summer, they were inseparable, appearing together at the Venice Film Festival and the Deauville Film Festival.

In September, they were out on one of George's motorcycles, when a car slammed into them. George broke a rib and Sarah, two toes. Although bruised and battered, the couple came through the incident with their relationship apparently unscathed and, inevitably, before the year was out, rumours were circulating that they were engaged. Predictably, whenever this was put to him, George issued a blank denial and it seemed that he was perfectly happy to leave things as they were. Like so many of George's previous relationships, however, the romance was destined not to last for long. The couple were to go their separate ways in May 2008.

On 27 August, George started work on a starring role in the latest Coen Brothers film, *Burn After Reading*, in which he plays "Harry Pfarrer" opposite Brad Pitt, Tilda Swinton, John Malkovich and Frances McDrormand. The film tells the story of a CIA agent who loses a disc containing his memoirs. The disc falls into the clutches of two gym employees. George has spoken of it as the third time he plays an 'idiot' for the Coen brothers. The shoot wrapped on 30 October 2007.

Days into that shoot, *Michael Clayton* premiered at the Venice Film Festival on 31 August. It later opened at cinemas on 5 October. The film went on to gross $49 million in the U.S. and a further $40 million worldwide.

Reviews were strong. *Variety* said, "If George Clooney's recent choices have oscillated between serious showcases (think *Syriana*) and moneymaking endeavours (the *Ocean's* series), this falls squarely into the former camp, presenting Warner Bros. with a classy but difficult to market, no-frills, few-thrills thriller." *The Los Angeles Times* called it "a smart and suspenseful legal thriller". *The Guardian* said, "As a corporate paranoia movie, *Michael Clayton* has something in common with Michael Mann's *The Insider* and at a further remove with Coppola's *The Conversation*."

Much of the remainder of 2007 was devoted to preparing *Leatherheads* for release, although George also found time to serve as executive producer and narrator for a documentary about the Darfur crisis, *Sand and Sorrow*, directed by Paul Freedman.

The film made its TV premiere on HBO in December 2007. On top of that, he also lent his voice to the animated film, *The Fantastic Mr Fox*. His part in the film is "Mr Fox".

At the turn of 2008, *Michael Clayton* was nominated for four awards in the Golden Globes: "Best Motion Picture Drama", "Best Performance by an Actor in a Motion Picture Drama" (George), "Best Performance by an Actor in a Supporting Role in a Motion Picture" (Tom Wilkinson) and "Best Performance by an Actress in a Supporting Role in a Motion Picture" (Tilda Swinton). Despite the excitement, the film scooped no awards that evening.

In January 2008, George's political activities and humanitarian efforts were recognised when he was designated a United Nations Messenger of Peace. No sooner had the title been assigned, than he was again visiting Chad and the troubled Darfur region of Sudan.

He had recently been asked repeatedly if he might consider running for political office, as his great grandfather and father had both done. In typically self-deprecatory fashion, George told one astonished reporter, "I couldn't run for office. I've slept with far too many women, I've done too many drugs and I've been to too many parties."

When the 79th Academy Awards

Left: George with Renee Zellweger at the *Leatherheads* London premiere when he also took the time to visit 10 Downing Street for talks with British Prime Minister Gordon Brown about Darfur.

ceremony came around, George was
once more in the audience. He had been
nominated for the "Best Performance by
an Actor in a Leading Role" award for
his work on *Michael Clayton*. He didn't
win. The film only picked up one award
– Tilda Swinton scooped the prize for
"Best Performance by an Actress in a
Supporting Role" category.

On Monday 24 March, George brought
the premiere of *Leatherheads* to Maysville,
Kentucky. It was the first time the town
had hosted a film premiere event since
George's Aunt, Rosemary Clooney, was
in town for the premiere of her big screen
debut, *The Stars Are Singing*, at the Russell
Theater in 1953. It was a moving moment,
George returning to the town where his
great-grandfather had once been mayor,
where his family roots lay.

According to *The Cincinnati Enquirer*,
George told fans, as he and co-star Renee
Zelleger worked the red carpet outside the
Washington Opera House Theater, "We've
had marriages, weddings and funerals
here, for one hundred years. This is home
for us. We're very proud to bring it full
circle. As Rosemary said, fifty five years
ago, it's nice to be home again."

Tickets for the event were limited to
approximately 300. The Opera House
Theater has 450 seats, but camera
projector equipment took up some of
that seat space. Maysville Assistant Police
Chief Ron Rice estimated the crowd at
slightly more than 2,000.

On 4 April 2008, *Leatherheads* opened
at cinemas across the U.S. and to the
disappointment of Warner Bros, failed
to take the top spot from gambling film,
21, grossing only $13.5 million over its
opening weekend.

Reviews were tepid. Salon.com
contemplated, "Whatever possessed
George Clooney to make a comedy
about professional football circa 1925, an
era when professional football, at least as
we know it now, barely existed? It's hard
to imagine who, if anyone, could care
about such a subject."

The San Francisco Chronicle displayed
the same indifference; "Leatherheads is
not that good a movie and yet it would
be hard to enjoy saying anything nasty
about it. Imagine a really nice, jolly, genial
person with a mild, intermittent hygiene
problem. This movie is a little like that."

In London, promoting *Leatherheads*,
George made a surprise appearance at
No. 10 Downing Street, where he met
with British Prime Minister, Gordon
Brown, on Tuesday 8 April, to discuss
the Darfur crisis.

And then George was onto preparing
the next slew of projects, constantly
driven by that ever-present fear that
one day the work might simply dry up.
Never mind that he'd be promoting
Leatherheads for the first half of 2008.
Never mind that *Burn After Reading*
would open at cinemas in Autumn 2008
and *The Fantastic Mr Fox* in late 2009.

George is always peering around the
corner, always anticipating the next
new porject, making himself one of the
busiest men in Hollywood. Still working
every hour he has. Still stubbornly single.
Still the toast of Hollywood. Still one of
the finest actors of his generation. Still a
savvy producer. Still a talented director.

So what of the future? Will he ever
stop? Or will he carry on like his Aunt
Rosemary and his father, Nick, working
through his old age, perhaps even until
he drops?

"The way you want to do it is like Cary
Grant. Have a successful career, then in
1966, decide you're looking too old, leave
the movies and never look back. Then at
80 years old have a stroke and drop dead.
That's perfect."

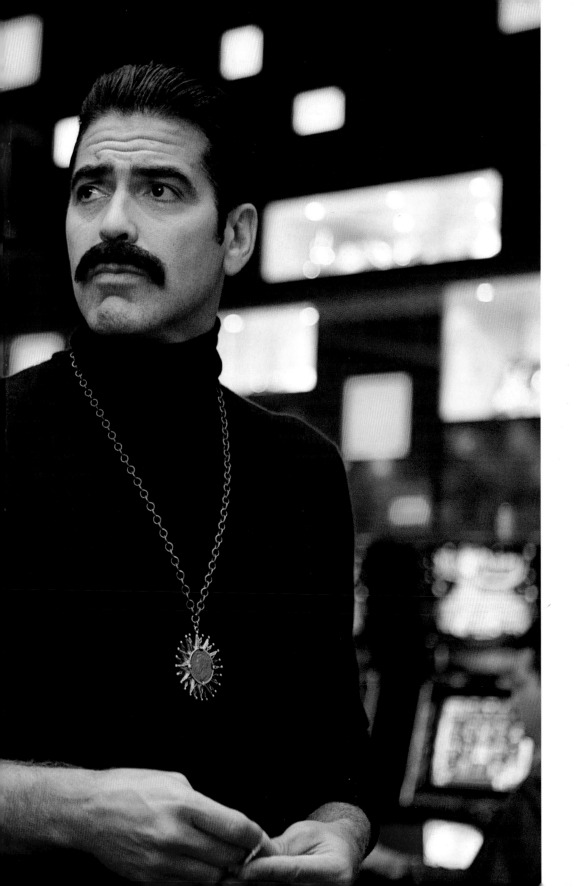

RESEARCH CREDITS

Articles from the following periodicals, wire services and websites assisted the researching of this book: *USA Today*, *The Guardian*, *The Chicago Sun Times*, *TV Guide*, *The Sunday Times*, *The Washington Post*, *The Village Voice*, *Rolling Stone*, *Esquire*, *Variety*, *The Observer*, *Reuters*, *The Independent*, Wenn, Splicedwire, *Time*, CNN, *Playboy*, *Parade*, *The San Francisco Chronicle*, *The Cincinnati Enquirer*, *The Sunday Mirror*, *GQ*, *Empire*, *The New Yorker*, *The Daily Mail*, *The New York Times*, Salon.com, The Clooney Network.

The publishers would like to thank the following sources for their kind permission to reproduce the pictures in this book.

AKG-Images: /© Warner Bros/Album: 86

Commuter Cars: 143

Corbis: /Bettmann: 10, 15; /Rufus F. Folkks: 157; / Kipa: 57; /Neal Preston: 34; /Frank Tapper/Corbis SYGMA: 85; /Jim Young/Reuters: 6

Flickr: 19

Getty Images: /56; /Stephanie Diani: 24; /Amro Maraghi/AFP: 144; /Online USA: 58, 60; /Jim Smeal: 25tl, 25, 35, 67

PA Photos: /AP: 18; /Richard Drew/AP: 141; / Starmax/Allaction.co.uk: 130; /Sherren Zorba/AP: 140

Photos 12: /Collection Cinema: 4-5, 9t, 59, 65, 66, 68, 74, 75, 76, 77, 79, 81, 90, 91, 93, 95, 98, 103, 106, 110, 114, 119, 123, 127, 129, 135, 136, 142, 153, 158-159

Picture Desk: /The Kobal Collection: 26, 42, 52

Rex Features: 99, 104; /© 20th Century Fox/Everett Collection: 72; /© ABC Inc/Everett Collection: 16, 41; /Corollalanza: 92; /Embassy/Everett Collection: 30; /Everett Collection: 9br, 21, 27, 28, 32, 36-37, 38, 40, 44, 63, 70, 78, 82, 83, 88, 97; /Globe Photos: 13; / KPA/Zuma: 151; /Dave Lewis: 61; /© MGM/Everett Collection: 43; /NBCU Photobank: 8, 14, 22, 29, 31, 45, 49, 50, 55; /© New World/Everett Collection: 33; / Alex Oliveira: 73; /Patrick Rideaux: 20; /Tim Rooke: 154; /Ron Sachs: 113; /Takashi Seida/Miramax Films: 108, 109, 117; /Sipa Press: 12, 69, 100, 138, 145; / SNAP: 17, 64; /© Universal/Everett Collection: 111, 118, 147, 148-149; /© Warner Bros/Everett Collection: 46-47, 96, 120, 122, 131, 133, 137

Topfoto.co.uk: 124

Every effort has been made to acknowledge correctly and contact the source and/copyright holder of each picture, and Carlton Books Limited apologises for any unintentional errors or omissions which will be corrected in future editions of this book.

Previous spread: An unfamiliar look for George, in disguise for *Ocean's Thirteen*.